"I can think of few things that the contemporary church needs to recover as much as the ancient practice of lectio divina. In my view it is the primary mode by which we are to receive Scripture. The focus of this series is rightly on the biblical text itself, and the commentary and questions push us back to the text to listen for God's address. My hope is that this well-written and accessible tool will assist readers in the practice of lectio divina."

—**Craig Bartholomew**, coauthor, *The Drama of Scripture*

"Stephen Binz has done an admirable job of introducing his readers to the process of lectio divina and immersing them in it. Through teaching the practice of this ancient way of studying the Bible, this series of Scripture studies will recharge and deepen the faith and lives of many, who thereafter will use the art for private devotions and/or in small groups. I heartily recommend this series to individuals and churches who want to join in the spirited revival of Christianity in our time!"

—**Marva J. Dawn**, Regent College

"At their recent Synod the world's Catholic bishops recommended lectio divina to all Christ's disciples, for prayerfully reading and making God's Word one's spiritual nourishment follows well-trod paths in the Christian tradition. Stephen Binz guides us on these paths in his Ancient-Future Bible Study series. I am pleased to recommend this project with enthusiasm."

—**Terrence Prendergast, SJ**, Archbishop of Ottawa

"Lectio divina, despite its centuries-long use, is still little known outside of monastic and academic settings. Ancient-Future Bible Study, a project that does great credit to Brazos Press, has in mind to correct that historical defect in Christian piety."

—**Patrick Henry Reardon**, author, *Creation and the Patriarchal Histories*

"Ancient-Future Bible Study brings a centuries-old approach to Scripture and prayer into the twenty-first century, providing sound commentary, thoughtful insights, and meaningful suggestions for personal reflection and meditation. Stephen Binz invites us to open our minds and hearts to the transforming power of God's Word. Under his guidance, the wisdom of the Bible comes vividly to life."

—**Carl McColman**, author, *The Big Book of Christian Mysticism*

"Stephen Binz has a knack for popularizing the Bible. His latest series, Ancient-Future Bible Study, demonstrates once more his ability to give people sound guidance as they read the Bible. I am happy to warmly recommend this modern application of the ancient method of lectio divina—the once and future way to read the Bible prayerfully—centered on fascinating characters from the Old and New Testaments."

—Fr. Ronald D. Witherup, author, *The Bible Companion*

"A method of Bible study that has a long and celebrated history in the church is given renewed momentum with this series. The goal here is more than instruction. The five movements of lectio divina are an invitation to immerse oneself in the riches of our biblical tradition and to give flesh to that tradition in our daily lives. This series will be a wonderful aid for the development of one's spiritual life."

—Dianne Bergant, CSA, Catholic Theological Union

"This series is a wonderful gift for the church in late modernity. In an era of twittered attention, we have inculcated all sorts of bad reading habits that we then bring to Scripture. The Ancient-Future Bible Study prescribes a counter-formative regimen: the personal and communal practice of lectio divina or 'sacred reading.' For some this will be a strange, new practice; but it will quickly feel as natural as breathing. So find some friends, take up this series, and read anew!"

—James K. A. Smith, Calvin College; author, *Desiring the Kingdom: Worship, Worldview, and Cultural Formation*

"Stephen Binz's new series allows us to put down the commentaries and word studies and let the beautiful poignancy of the text seep into our souls, all with the aid of the Holy Spirit. I heartily recommend it."

—Tony Jones, Solomon's Porch, Minneapolis; author, *The New Christians: Dispatches from the Emergent Frontier*

"Stephen Binz, a responsible biblical scholar and experienced pastor, has undertaken the important project of leading non-professional but committed readers of the Bible into a spiritually enlivening encounter with the biblical text through engagement with some of the fascinating characters who people its pages. Anyone yearning to pray the biblical text will find this series a useful companion."

—Sandra M. Schneiders, Jesuit School of Theology

ANCIENT-FUTURE BIBLE STUDY

PETER

Fisherman and Shepherd of the Church

STEPHEN J. BINZ

Brazos Press

a division of Baker Publishing Group
Grand Rapids, Michigan

© 2011 by Stephen J. Binz

Published by Brazos Press
a division of Baker Publishing Group
P.O. Box 6287, Grand Rapids, MI 49516-6287
www.brazospress.com

Printed in the United States of America

Library of Congress Cataloging-in-Publication Data

Binz, Stephen J., 1955–
    Peter : fisherman and shepherd of the church / Stephen J. Binz.
       p.   cm. — (Ancient-future Bible study)
    ISBN 978-1-58743-279-8 (pbk.)
      1. Peter, the Apostle, Saint—Textbooks. 2. Bible. N.T.—Biography—Textbooks.
    I. Title. II. Series.
    BS2515.B49 2011
    225.9′2—dc22
                                      2010029534

Some content from "Welcome to Ancient-Future Bible Study" originally appeared in Stephen J. Binz, *Conversing with God in Scripture: A Contemporary Approach to Lectio Divina* (Ijamsville, MD: The Word Among Us Press, 2008).

11   12   13   14   15   16   17   7 6 5 4 3 2 1

Contents

Acknowledgments

For the past several years my work has focused on making connections between ancient practices and contemporary experiences. My speaking, writing, and counseling under the trademark Bridge-Building Opportunities has emphasized the link between past and present, East and West, time-honored tradition and progressive renewal in the fields of biblical theology, Christian spirituality, and personal growth.

When I discovered the mission of Brazos Press, I felt that I had found a new home. By its own definition, Brazos Press is "staked on the discernment that while various existing Christian categories (liberal and conservative, mainline and evangelical, even Catholic and Protestant) prove increasingly unserviceable, there is at the same time occurring a robust renewal of classical, orthodox Christianity across many of the old lines or borders." This is a publisher that is eager to cross boundaries, build bridges, and extend the vital roots of the ancient Christian tradition into the twenty-first century.

I am grateful to Jim Kinney, associate publisher and editorial director of Baker Academic and Brazos Press, for supporting my work. Lisa Ann Cockrel, editor for this series, has masterfully guided these books through the editorial process and improved this work with her many ideas. I also appreciate the skillful work of Lisa Beth Anderson, Rodney Clapp, Steve Ayers, BJ Heyboer, Jeremy Wells, Caitlin Mackenzie, and the whole Brazos team for their efforts to refine and promote this project.

The term "Ancient-Future" seems to perfectly express the bridge between ancient wisdom and future possibilities that I want to create in this series. The term is applied in a number of other spheres to emphasize a blending of tradition and innovation. In the arts, ancient-future music and dance is created through fusing centuries-old traditions with contemporary genres and technology. By learning from the world's great traditions and ancient practices, artists create cross-cultural expressions that are richly profound yet also widely appealing.

I am particularly indebted to the work of the late Robert Webber, many of whose books use the term "Ancient-Future" to express his mission of drawing wisdom from the past and translating those insights into the present and future life of the church, its faith, worship, ministry, and spirituality. In his own words: "My argument is that the era of the early church (AD 100–500), and particularly the second century, contains insights which evangelicals need to recover." This series resonates with his outstanding work and hopefully, in some small way, will honor his memory and continue his vision.

Finally, I am grateful to all my friends and colleagues in the field of biblical studies and to all pastors, lay ministers, and church volunteers who are dedicated to an anciently rooted and forward-looking Christianity. Particularly I want to express my appreciation to my wife Pamela, a professor of music, for the loving support and inspiration she constantly offers to me.

Welcome to Ancient-Future Bible Study

Ancient-Future Bible Study unites contemporary study of the Bible with an experience of the church's most ancient way of reading Scripture, *lectio divina*. By combining the old and the new in a fertile synthesis, this study helps modern people encounter the *sacra pagina*, the inspired text, as God intends it for the church. Through solid historical and literary study and the time-honored practice of lectio divina, the mind and the heart are brought into an experience of God through a careful and prayerful reading of the biblical texts.

As the Word of its divine author, the Bible is not just a literary anthology of ancient texts; it is inspired literature addressed to God's people. God intends the sacred texts to move from our heads to the depths of our hearts and to form us as a new people living in God's reign. Ancient-Future Bible Study guides readers to listen to Scripture within the tradition and scholarship of the church in order to unleash its life-changing potential.

The ancient art of lectio divina is rooted in the Jewish tradition of Jesus, and it was nourished through the desert spirituality of the early centuries, the patristic writers of the ancient church, and the monastic tradition through the ages. In our day, lectio divina is experiencing a worldwide revival as Christians are returning to age-old wisdom to experience the Scriptures in a deeper and more complete way.

As you experience Ancient-Future Bible Study, you will realize how the church's long tradition of biblical study, reflection, prayer, discernment, and contemplative action can enrich your discipleship. You will learn how to dispose yourself to be formed by the Word of God as you join with the array of men and women through the ages whose lives have been transformed by that same living Word.

Reasons for Studying the Bible

Most often people study the Bible for one of three reasons. First, they study for information and knowledge. This usually includes a search for historical facts, doctrinal truths, and moral guidance. Second, they study to find advice for solving a personal need or getting through a life crisis. This usually involves seeking out lists of specific passages that speak to the particular needs of the moment. Third, they study so they can defend their faith and witness to others. This usually consists of choosing selected passages to remember and quote, so they can argue for a particular approach to faith or help lead others toward the truth. While all of these objectives can lead to good results, their accomplishments are always limited and partial.

The most complete reason for studying Scripture is for the purpose of encountering the living God through the sacred text. This divine encounter leads not just to more information and advice but to a deeply rooted transformation of life. The inspired Word evokes a spiritual transformation within the lives of those who allow God's Word to do its true work, urging us to personal growth in Christ and fuller discipleship.

For Scripture to have its deepest effects in us we must approach the text with humility, reverence, and expectation. As we receive its revelation and understand its truth, Scripture has the ability to gradually change our minds and mold our hearts. Unlike any other literature, the words of the Bible can renew our lives when we approach the text as an encounter with its divine author.

The Indwelling of the Holy Spirit

The Bible was written under the inspiration of the Holy Spirit. God's "breathing in," acting in union with the human authors of the texts, makes the Scriptures the Word of the living God. Because God is the primary author of the Bible, we can be assured that the texts have a power that transcends that of any other spiritual reading.

God's inspiration of the biblical books does not refer only to a past reality, to the historical time in which the biblical authors were guided to write the texts. Rather, the work of God's Spirit is an ongoing reality within the inspired books. The sacred texts remain inspired; they are forever permeated with divine breath and are filled now with the Spirit of God.

This understanding of the Spirit's enduring and ongoing presence in the biblical texts is the foundation of lectio divina. Through the Holy Spirit, God addresses his Word to us here and now through the ancient text. Because of the indwelling Spirit, the Word is alive and has the power to transform us. The Word of God is charged with creative power to change and renew us from within.

The Movements of Lectio Divina

Lectio divina (LEK-tsee-oh dih-VEEN-ah) is best translated, though incompletely, as "sacred reading." Its revitalization, like the renewal of other spiritual practices from the early church, is becoming a means of deep spiritual growth for people today. Lectio divina helps us return to the most ancient understanding of the sacredness of the inspired text. The Bible is not like a textbook, used for looking up factual documentation, nor is it like a manual, describing a how-to method for solving problems. Rather, it is a means of forming our life in God and joining us to the story of God's people.

The process of lectio divina appeals not only to our minds but also to our imaginations and feelings. We seek to understand and experience Scripture as a real communication, as God personally addressing us. In practicing lectio divina, we get caught up in the literature and learn to love the text itself; we read it reflectively, lingering over it, and let it reach the depths of our hearts. We let go of our own agenda and expectations, gradually opening ourselves to what God wants us to experience through the sacred page.

There is no single method for the practice of lectio divina. It is not a rigid step-by-step system for encountering God in biblical passages. The spiritual masters of the early church distrusted methods of prayer and spiritual practice that were too rigidly defined, wishing instead to cultivate the freedom necessary to respond to the Spirit's promptings. Lectio divina aims toward a holistic experience of Scripture, incorporating our intellects, feelings, and actions.

Ancient-Future Bible Study incorporates five "movements." Comparable to the movements in a classical work of music, each movement has its own characteristics and can even be practiced independently of the others. There is plenty of room for personal interpretation within the tradition. Individually and together, lectio, meditatio, oratio, contemplatio, and operatio contribute to the full experience of lectio divina.

Pronunciation Guide

Lectio—LEK-tsee-oh
Meditatio—meh-dih-TAH-tsee-oh
Oratio—oh-RAH-tsee-oh
Contemplatio—con-tem-PLAH-tsee-oh
Operatio—oh-peh-RAH-tsee-oh

Lectio—*Reading the Text with a Listening Ear*

Lectio is more than ordinary reading. It might best be described as listening deeply—what St. Benedict in the sixth century described as hearing "with the ear of our heart." This listening requires that we try to receive God's Word with as little prejudgment as possible, as if we were hearing it for the first time. Lectio urges us to create a space within us for the new wisdom and understanding God wants to give us through the sacred page.

Saint Ambrose in the fourth century urged readers to avoid the tendency to read large passages in haste: "We should read not in agitation, but in calm; not hurriedly, but slowly, a few words at a time, pausing in attentive reflection. . . . Then the readers will experience their ability to enkindle the ardor of prayer." We might even consider returning to the ancient practice of reading texts aloud in order to instill within ourselves the sense of reading Scripture as a deep listening.

The essential question to ask in this first movement is, "What does the text say and what does it mean?" The Jewish rabbis and the church's patristic writers show us that there is no clear distinction between studying and praying Scripture. The more we come to understand the text with our minds, the more we are capable of being changed by the text. Wrestling with the text and seeking to comprehend its meaning is an important part of encountering God there and being changed by that encounter.

Once we've read the text slowly and carefully, Ancient-Future Bible Study invites us to learn from the commentary that follows the biblical passage. This too is part of listening to the text, only here we listen with the understanding of the church and with some basic insights of biblical scholarship. This listening to the text, with its multiple layers of meaning and rich history of interpretation, forms the foundation on which we experience the subsequent movements of lectio divina. We do what we can to make sure our reading of the text is faithful and true, so that we don't reduce God's revelation to our own imaginary constructions. On this firm basis, we construct the process of prayerfully encountering God's Word.

We might read the text as literature, looking at its words, metaphors, images, and characters. We could look at its structure and its literary form— is it poetry, parable, history, proverb, legal code, epic, or apocalypse? We should realize that God's truth is expressed in a variety of types of literature, each type expressing truth in a different way. The more we can comprehend something of the original historical, cultural, literary, and religious context of the passage, the better we will be able to probe all the potential the text can offer us.

In lectio, the words of Scripture become the means of God speaking to us. As God's Spirit guided the human authors to express the truth that God wished to entrust to the Scriptures, God also guides us through that same Spirit as we read the Bible as God's Word to us.

Meditatio—*Reflecting on the Meaning and Message of the Text*

The question to ask in this movement is, "What does the text say to me and mean to me?" Meditatio aims to bring the biblical passage into the sphere of my own life as I seek to understand how the Scripture passage speaks to me today.

Though there is a wide gap of time, language, and culture between the world of the biblical writers and our own world, meditatio bridges that gap. By reflecting on the text as well as on our own experiences, thoughts, challenges, and questions, we can grow in our understanding that God is speaking personally to us through the scriptural text. This reflection forms connections between the text of yesterday and the today of our lives.

Ancient-Future Bible Study stimulates meditatio through the use of questions for reflection. These questions encourage a deeper and more personal consideration of the text. They challenge the reader to create a dialogue between the ancient text and life today. As the Word of God, the Bible has a richness of meaning that can be discovered in every age and every culture. It has a particular message that can be received by everyone who listens to God's Word in the context of daily experiences and in the same Spirit in which it was written.

The more we meditate on God's Word, the more it seeps into our lives and saturates our thoughts and feelings. Meditatio allows the dynamic Word of God to so penetrate our lives that it truly infuses our minds and hearts and we begin to embody its truth and its goodness.

Oratio—*Praying in Response to God's Word*

Careful lectio and reflective meditatio open the way for God to enter into our hearts and inflame them with the grace of his love. There, at the core of our being, we naturally want to respond to the One whose voice we have heard. Oratio is our prayerful response to God's Word.

Lectio divina is fundamentally a dialogue with God, a gentle oscillation between listening to God and responding to him in prayer. When we recognize that God has offered us a message that is unique to our own lives—an insight, a challenge, a comfort, a call—we arrive at the moment when we must ask ourselves, "Now what am I going to say in response to God?" This is the moment of prayer.

Oratio is not just any form of prayer. It is born from the experience of listening to God in Scripture. The biblical words we have heard and reflected on become the words of our prayer. The style and vocabulary of our prayer are enriched through the inspired words of the biblical tradition. Whether our oratio is an act of praise or thanksgiving, of petition or repentance, we pray in response to what we have heard. Our prayers no longer consist of mechanically repeated formulas. Rather, they resonate with the faith, hope, and love that animated the people of the Bible in their journey with God.

Ancient-Future Bible Study offers examples of this type of prayer. After each session of lectio and meditatio, we are encouraged to continue in intimate prayer to God, melding the words, images, and sentiments of the biblical text with personal thoughts, feelings, and desires arising from the heart.

Contemplatio—*Quietly Resting in God*

Both oratio and contemplatio are forms of prayer. Oratio is our active, word-filled prayer in response to God's Word. Contemplatio is prayer without words. It is the response to God that remains after words are no longer necessary or helpful. It is simply enjoying the experience of quietly being in God's presence.

Contemplatio requires that we let go of any effort to be in charge of the process. When we feel God drawing us into a deeper awareness of his divine presence, we gradually abandon our intellectual activity and let ourselves be wooed into God's embrace. We no longer have to think or reason, listen or speak. The experience resembles that of lovers holding each other in wordless silence or of a sleeping child resting in the arms of his or her mother.

Though we may think the movement of contemplatio is passive and uneventful, it is not. When we humbly expose our heart, the center of our being, to God, what happens within us during those moments is really not up to us. In contrast to the rapid, noisy communication of our technological world, quiet, receptive stillness is the atmosphere in which the most important communication occurs. God's grace is truly at work in those moments, and the Holy Spirit is changing us without our direct knowledge or understanding.

Operatio—*Faithful Witness in Daily Life*

After reading, reflecting, and praying over a scriptural passage, we should be impacted in a way that makes a difference in our daily lives. Operatio is our lived response to the biblical text. The question operatio calls forth from us is, "How can I live out the Word of God that I have heard in my heart?"

We cannot prayerfully read Scripture without being changed in some specific way. As we deepen our relationship with God through the movements of lectio divina, our actions become vehicles of his presence to others. We become channels of God's compassion and mercy, becoming "doers of the word, and not merely hearers" (James 1:22), bringing about God's loving purposes in our daily lives.

Contemplatio and operatio should not be totally distinct and separate. Their impulses grow together in the heart of one who prayerfully reads Scripture. Contemplatio does not separate us from the world, and operatio is not genuine unless it grows out of contemplative reflection. Apart from contemplatio, operatio could become superficial pragmatism.

The Bible should never be viewed as simply a collection of maxims to be put into practice. Rarely does Scripture offer us concrete details about what to do in specific situations. Our human reason and experience must always accompany our prayerful discernment as we decide how to live out the Word of God. Listening, reflection, prayer, and contemplation are all necessary components from which flows the operatio of Christian discipleship. Lectio divina helps us become contemplative activists and active contemplatives.

The Essence of Lectio Divina

The movements of lectio divina are more like the colors of a rainbow than clearly defined stages. They overlap, blending into one another, ebbing and flowing according to the rhythm of the divine Spirit and the human heart. The five movements used in Ancient-Future Bible Study are part of a rich tradition, though additional phases are sometimes found in other historical forms of the practice: studium (study), cogitatio (reflection), consolatio (comfort), discretio (discernment), deliberatio (decision making), compassio (compassion), and actio (action).

While the most ancient practice of lectio divina is not a rigid system of biblical reflection, nor does its method require any particular steps, there are a few characteristics that identify the authentic practice of lectio divina:

‡ *Lectio divina is a personal encounter with God through Scripture.* The text itself is a gateway to God. Through the inspired Scripture, we meet the God who loves us and desires our response.

‡ *Lectio divina establishes a dialogue between the reader of Scripture and God.* The attentive reader listens to God through the text and responds to God in heartfelt prayer. The heart of lectio divina is this gentle conversation with God.

‡ *Lectio divina creates a heart-to-heart intimacy with God.* In the Bible, the heart is a person's innermost core, the place from which one's deepest longings, motivations, decisions, memories, and desires arise. The prayerful reader responds to God's Word with the whole heart and thereby grows in a relationship with God at the deepest level of intimacy.

‡ *Lectio divina leads to contemplation and action.* There is a moment in all true love that leads to a level of communication too deep for words. Prayerful reading inevitably leads to that deepest form of communication with God, which is loving silence. In addition, all true love must be expressed in action. Eventually words become inadequate, and love must be demonstrated in deeds arising from a changed heart.

The Word of God and its power to change us are gifts from God that we must accept into our lives. In order to receive the gift of divine intimacy, we must create the necessary conditions within us. Openheartedness, faithfulness, and expectation will enable us to more readily listen and receive. The more we remove the obstacles in the way—our inner resistance, our fear of intimacy, our impatient awareness of time, our desire to control the process, and our self-concern—the more we can expect Scripture to transform our lives.

Sometimes the changes are remarkable; more often they are subtle. We gradually become aware that the fruit of studying the Bible is the fruit of the Spirit: "love, joy, peace, patience, kindness, generosity, faithfulness, gentleness, and self-control" (Gal. 5:22–23). When we begin to notice this fruit in the way we live each day, we will know that the Word of God is working within us.

Your Personal Practice of Ancient-Future Bible Study

‡ This study is designed to provide maximum flexibility so that you can make lectio divina a regular part of your life according to your circum-

stances. If you are able to make the time in your daily schedule, you will want to reflect on one chapter each day. If not, you may select three weekdays to read three chapters per week. Or if your weekends are more leisurely, you may choose to reflect on two chapters per weekend.

‡ Reading Plan #1—30 days/5 weeks
  • Engage six lessons per week

‡ Reading Plan #2—60 days/10 weeks
  • Engage three lessons per week

‡ Reading Plan #3—90 days/15 weeks
  • Engage two lessons per weekend

‡ Whatever pace you choose for your practice of lectio divina, try to find a regular time during the day that can become a pattern for you. Choose a quiet and comfortable place where you will be undisturbed during the time of your lectio divina.

‡ During your regular time for lectio divina, try to rid yourself of as many distractions as possible. Before you begin reading the Bible, take time to call upon the Holy Spirit for guidance. Light a candle, ring a chime, kiss the Bible, or do some other action that will designate these moments as sacred time.

‡ Read the biblical text slowly and carefully. Read the passage in another translation, if you wish, to help your understanding. Don't hesitate to mark up this book with highlights, underlining, circles, or whatever will help you pay attention and remember the text and commentary.

‡ Follow the movements of lectio divina outlined in each section. Realize that this is only a tentative guide for the more important movements of God's Spirit within you. Write out your responses to the questions provided. The questions following the lectio are objective questions synthesizing your reading of the text and commentary. Those under meditatio are more personal questions, requiring thoughtful reflection. Try also to write comments on the sections of oratio, contemplatio, and operatio, according to the suggestions provided. The very act of writ-

ing will help you clarify your thoughts, bring new insights, and amplify your understanding.

✝ Approach your lectio divina with expectancy, trusting that God will indeed work deeply within you through his Word. Through this experience, know that you are placing yourself within a long procession of God's people through the ages who have allowed themselves to be transformed through lectio divina.

✝ Finally, try to be accountable to at least one other person for your regular practice of lectio divina. Tell a spouse, friend, spiritual director, or minister about your experience in order to receive their encouragement and affirmation.

Bringing Ancient-Future Bible Study to Churches

Throughout the history of salvation, God's Word has been directed first and foremost to a community, not just to individuals. The people of Israel, the community of disciples, and the early church were the recipients of God's self-communication expressed in the Scriptures. For this reason, studying the Bible in the context of a community of faith can deepen and enrich our individual experience.

Churches and other faith communities may choose to adopt Ancient-Future Bible Study and encourage its use in a variety of ways. Since this Bible study is ideally suited both for personal use by individuals and for communal practice, congregations are able to respect the many ways people desire to make Scripture a priority in their lives. By encouraging an array of options for participation, churches will increase the number of people in the congregation who are making reading and reflection on the Bible a regular part of their lives in Christ.

Collatio—The Communal Practice of Lectio Divina

The ancient term for the communal practice of lectio divina is collatio (coh-LAH-tsee-oh), a term that originally meant "a bringing together, interchange, or discussion." Its aim is building up a spiritual community around the Word of God. Collatio began in an age when books were rare and precious. Today, when everyone may have their own Bible, collatio may be practiced in many different ways.

Here are some ways of building up a faith community with Ancient-Future Bible Study:

‡ Offer this study to people who want to participate only on their own. Respect the fact that many people don't have the time or desire to gather with others. Instead they can be encouraged to read and reflect on their own with the prayerful support of the whole community.

‡ Promote the formation of informal groups made up of family, friends, neighbors, or work associates.

‡ Facilitate usage of the study through online communities or social networks. Online group members might want to commit themselves to sending an email or text message to the group offering their insights after reflecting on each Scripture passage.

‡ Set up small groups that meet regularly at church facilities or in homes. These groups may meet at different times throughout the week to offer convenient options for people in different circumstances. Groups could be made up of people with obvious connections: young adults, retired seniors, parents with young children, professionals, couples, etc. These groupings may encourage a deeper level of personal reflection among members.

Biblical reading and reflection on a regular basis is an important part of Christian discipleship. Every member of our congregations should be encouraged to make Bible reading and reflection a regular part of their lives. This is best accomplished when pastoral leadership promotes this practice and when people are personally invited to participate. When practicing lectio divina within a community of faith, we learn to place our own lives into the story of God's people throughout the ages.

Further Help for Groups

‡ Additional information for facilitating small groups with Ancient-Future Bible Study may be found starting on page 159 of this book.

✝ Since Ancient-Future Bible Study is divided into units of six lessons, motivated groups may choose to study five lessons per week on their own, with a weekly group session discussing insights from the daily lessons and practicing the sixth lesson of the week in the group.

✝ Groups with less daily time to study may divide the six lessons in half, choosing to study two lessons per week on their own, with a weekly group session discussing insights from the daily lessons and practicing the third lesson of the week in the group.

✝ The practice of lectio divina for each lesson will take about thirty minutes for an individual. Those who wish to spend extended time in reflection and prayer should allow for more time. The group session, using the suggestions at the back of this book, will take about ninety minutes.

✝ Additional information about Ancient-Future Bible Study, with descriptions of published and upcoming studies, may be found online at www .brazospress.com/ancientfuturebiblestudy. You can also connect to the series and its author on Facebook.

Introduction to *Peter: Fisherman and Shepherd of the Church*

The life of Peter is one of the most fascinating and inspiring in the Bible. He was an ordinary Jewish fisherman, but through his experiences with Jesus of Nazareth, he became one of the key figures in the history of the world. Yet despite his fame, his many strengths and weaknesses and his richly developed and complex personality in the biblical narratives make him thoroughly accessible to the average Christian. For anyone seeking to know and walk with Jesus Christ, Peter is both a brother and a teacher.

When Jesus met Peter, he encountered a kindred spirit. Like Jesus, Peter had grown up in the Judaism of the Galilean synagogues and had probably participated in the annual pilgrimages to Jerusalem. He experienced with Jesus the world of the Galilean peasants, craftsmen, fishermen, and farmers. Peter's friendship with Jesus was genuine, and his relationship to Jesus's burgeoning movement was unique.

Peter is easily the most prominent of Jesus's disciples. He appears in the Gospels more frequently than all the other disciples combined. Peter receives special attention in many situations during the life of Jesus, and he is often the spokesperson for the other disciples. He is the first called by Jesus and made a fisher of men and women, and in every list of Jesus's twelve disciples, his name appears first. He is the first to profess genuine faith in Jesus, always the first to answer Jesus, and named first by Paul as witness to Jesus's resurrection (1 Cor. 15:5). In the life of the early church, Peter exercises a clear primacy. He preaches the first sermon at Pentecost, converting thousands to belief in Christ; he performs the first recorded

1

miracle in the apostolic church, healing a crippled beggar in the name of Christ; and he is the first to convert a Gentile, opening the mission of the church to all people.

Yet, despite the distinctive role of Peter among the disciples, he seems to be a mass of contradictions. He confesses that Jesus is the Son of God then refuses to accept Jesus's mission as the suffering Messiah. Jesus appoints him as the rock foundation of his church, but Peter shows himself a stumbling block on Jesus's path to the cross. He bravely walks on the water at the direction of Jesus but then fearfully begins to sink like a stone. Peter reverently offers to erect tents on the mountain when Jesus appears in glory but falls asleep when Jesus asks him to watch with him in his grief. He promises to lay down his life for Jesus but that same night denies three times that he ever knew him. In the early days of the church, he risks his reputation to share the gospel with Gentiles but later refuses to eat with them in Antioch.

Peter is bold and cowardly, impulsive and fearful, filled with bravado yet weak, flawed, and sinful. In reading the Gospels, we see a wide range of responses, from his foolish bluster to his passionate commitment to Jesus. We witness Peter the disciple weeping in anguish after denying his master as well as the deliriously happy fisherman who jumps into the water and swims as fast as he can to meet his risen Lord.

Though Peter often fails to live up to his calling, because of his humility and repentance, he learns and grows in his discipleship through his failures. Peter never tries to minimize, justify, or rationalize his own mistakes, but he honestly confesses his sins and failings. The evangelists demonstrate that Peter's own merits and accomplishments do not create his heroic character; rather, he is defined in Christian history by what the love of Jesus wrought in him. Peter challenges us to confront the truth of our own brokenness so that God's grace can fashion us into the disciples Jesus calls us to be.

Questions to Consider

‡ Why does it seem that Peter is such a fascinating and inspiring biblical character? What do I hope to learn from his heroic life?

‡ Why did Jesus choose Peter to be his leading disciple rather than a learned and respected member of the religious establishment?

The Portrait of Peter in the New Testament

The presence of Peter cuts across the pages of the New Testament like that of no other disciple. He is mentioned so frequently that it would be impossible, in a study of this nature, to include every passage that mentions him. Each of the four Gospel writers portrays Peter from a slightly different perspective, and each includes his own additional material from the tradition of the primitive church. We will focus on the Gospel of Matthew, written for a mixed Jewish and Gentile community, and the Gospel of John, the latest of the four Gospels in its final form. For Peter's role in the church's early decades, we will turn to the Acts of the apostles, which shows Peter as the leader and chief spokesperson for the emerging church, and we will conclude by looking at a few brief passages from the letters of Paul and Peter.

The predominant biblical portrayals of Peter, as fisherman and shepherd of the church, are highlighted first in the Gospels. Though fishing is in his blood, Peter is invited by Jesus to leave his fishing boat and nets to follow him, becoming a fisher of people. This image of Peter presents him as Christ's missionary and evangelist. As he had lured fish into his nets, he now attracts men and women, inviting them into the great net of salvation cast out through the evangelizing work of the church. As a missionary, Peter proclaims the gospel in distant lands and, through the work of Christ's Spirit, helps extend the church of Christ from Jerusalem to the ends of the earth.

The other image of Peter, as shepherd of the church, depicts the chief apostle of Jesus as the pastor of God's flock. By supervising Christian communities, guarding the flock, warding off dangers, and leading the fold with care, Peter fulfills the task of tending the sheep left to him by the risen Lord. Following the example of Jesus, the Good Shepherd who calls his sheep by name and desires to bring in other sheep that do not belong to the fold, Peter pastors the flock of Jewish Christians and reaches out to offer the pasture of salvation even to the Gentiles. Like his master who laid down his life for his sheep, Peter gives his life for the church, beginning in Jerusalem and ending with martyrdom in Rome.

In this study, we will follow Peter's experiences with Jesus and his struggles to be a faithful disciple. We will see him develop from a new follower of Jesus into a mature disciple through his years of ministry. Through the personal reflection and prayer stimulated by this study, we will grow in our understanding of Jesus and the great call we have received to faith and discipleship in him.

Questions to Consider

‡ What does the image of Peter as fisherman tell us about his role in the mission of Christ?

‡ How does the image of Peter as the church's shepherd express the qualities formed in Peter through the love of Jesus?

Peter, the Bridge Builder and Center of Unity

Peter was a bridge builder. As fisherman and shepherd of the church, Peter provided the first apostolic link between the earthly ministry of Jesus and the post-Easter church. After the death of Jesus on the cross, his disciples scattered in discouragement and fear. Yet, when Peter saw the risen Lord, he experienced forgiveness and returned to following Jesus. He reassembled the circle of disciples in Jerusalem and received the church's first converts, proclaiming that Jesus had poured out the Holy Spirit upon his church.

Peter was also a bridge builder among the church's early leadership. While Peter was the primary figure in the Jerusalem church from its earliest days, he left Jerusalem after his imprisonment and began his work as a missionary in other communities. After Peter's departure, it seems that James became the chief overseer of the Jerusalem church. Meanwhile,

Paul was testifying to increasing numbers of Gentiles coming into the church. In the ongoing dispute between Jewish and Gentile Christianity, the greatest source of tension within the expanding church, Peter took a centrist position, reconciling the polar positions of James, representing Jewish Christians, and Paul, representing Gentile Christians. While deeply respectful of his Jewish roots, Peter also encouraged the mission of the church to reach out beyond the Jewish culture.

According to the renowned scholar James D. G. Dunn, Peter did more than any other to hold together the diversity of first-century Christianity. He established the bridge between the early church in Jerusalem and the ever-widening church scattered throughout the Roman Empire. Peter, thus, became the focal point of unity for that worldwide community of faith that would soon describe itself as the one, holy, catholic, and apostolic church.

The New Testament gives us clues about the end of Peter's life, but it does not narrate his death. There is strong evidence that Peter was drawn to Rome late in his career. His role as a mediating centrist suggests that he could have played a crucial role in building bridges between the divided Jewish and Gentile house churches there as well. Evidence from archaeology and historical sources indicates that Peter died a martyr's death in Rome during the persecutions begun by Nero. The site of his martyrdom and tomb became a place of veneration for the early Christians.

Questions to Consider

‡ In what way was Peter a bridge builder between the conservative James and the liberal Paul? Why does the church need bridge builders today?

‡ Why was Peter's ministry of unity important for the early church? How might the model of Peter serve as a force for unity within Christianity today?

From Crumbled Failure to Rock of Strength

Listen to these challenging words that Jesus addressed to Peter at the Last Supper.

LUKE 22:31–32

[31]"Simon, Simon, listen! Satan has demanded to sift all of you like wheat, [32]but I have prayed for you that your own faith may not fail; and you, when once you have turned back, strengthen your brothers."

After letting these prophetic words sink in, continue searching for their significance in the ongoing ministry of Peter the apostle.

These brief verses from Luke's account of the Last Supper summarize the ordeal of Simon Peter's discipleship during the passion account and anticipate his role beyond the Gospel and into the life of Christ's church. Jesus speaks of three aspects of Peter's testing: his sifting by Satan, his turning back to following Jesus, and his role in strengthening his brothers.

Jesus says that Satan has demanded "to sift all of you like wheat" (v. 31), that is, to severely test the disciples for the purpose of destroying their faith. The devil has already taken Judas, and now he is attempting to take the other disciples too. Indeed, that very night Peter's fear will overpower his faith, and he will deny Jesus three times.

Jesus's plan for his community of disciples involves Peter's repentance and return to discipleship. Jesus assures Peter that he has prayed for him so that his faith will not collapse in the time of crisis. Though Peter will falter in faith, he will weep bitterly over his failing, marking the beginning of his turning back to Jesus.

In the remainder of his Gospel and in his second volume, the Acts of the Apostles, Luke demonstrates Peter's pivotal role among the other disciples in his ministry of strengthening them. Peter's complete return to Jesus is not brought about by his own initiative but through the sovereign initiative of his risen Lord. The disciples exclaim, "The Lord has risen indeed, and he has appeared to Simon!" (24:34). The strength of Peter's testimony convinces the others to join in affirming Jesus's resurrection. The Acts of the apostles shows that Peter gathers the disciples again as a community in Jerusalem and that he becomes the leading figure in the infant church.

Jesus's double address, "Simon, Simon" (v. 31), signals Jesus's particular concern for Simon Peter and his desire to assign a unique ministry to him. This is the only passage in Luke's Gospel that indicates why Jesus might have given Simon the name "Peter," a name that means "rock." Though Simon certainly did not act very rocklike during the passion of Jesus, through genuine repentance and the forgiveness of the risen Jesus, he becomes the rock of strength for the early church.

Meditatio

Reflect on the experiences of Peter in his failure, his repentance, and his strengthening ministry. Consider how he might be a friend and mentor in your discipleship.

‡ Jesus assured Peter of his prayers for him so that Peter's faith would not fail. How might this assurance of Jesus's prayers have helped Peter to get through his period of testing without abandoning his faith? In what way do I depend on prayer for my own strength in times of trial?

‡ Peter's experience of failure as a disciple enabled him later to be a better source of strength for others. In what way have I found strength for others through my experiences of failure?

Oratio

After listening to God's Word in Scripture, respond in prayer to God, who always listens to your voice.

Lord Jesus Christ, you chose Simon Peter as your disciple and prayed for him in times of trial. As the first among your stumbling disciples, he struggled with doubt and fear, failing you in your most desperate hour. Teach me, through the example of Peter's life, how to trust in you and depend on your grace. As I continue to listen, reflect, and pray these biblical texts of Peter's life, strengthen me and help me to be a source of strength for my brothers and sisters.

Continue to give voice to your heart . . .

Contemplatio

Jesus assured Peter of his prayers for him so that Peter's faith would not fail. Remain in peaceful quiet for a few minutes and be aware of Jesus's prayerful support of you. Feel the passionate care of Jesus for you.

Operatio

How can I best dedicate myself to the reflective study of these sacred texts of Peter over the coming weeks? What regular place and time could I choose for the quiet practice of lectio divina?

1

Peter's Call to Discipleship

Lectio

Realize that your encounter with the Scriptures is a sacred time. Prepare for this moment by closing off the distractions of the day and entering a space where you can listen to the scriptural text with focused attention.

MATTHEW 4:18–22

18As he walked by the Sea of Galilee, he saw two brothers, Simon, who is called Peter, and Andrew his brother, casting a net into the sea—for they were fishermen. 19And he said to them, "Follow me, and I will make you fish for people." 20Immediately they left their nets and followed him. 21As he went from there, he saw two other brothers, James son of Zebedee and his brother John, in the boat with their father Zebedee, mending their nets, and he called them. 22Immediately they left the boat and their father, and followed him.

Continue seeking to understand this text and its significance through the wisdom of the church's scholarship and tradition.

The life of the Galilee region was centered on its large lake. A number of dramatic scenes from Jesus's early ministry took place on or around this Sea of Galilee. The lake was thick with fishing boats, and the region prospered through its fishing industry. The fish were caught by casting a net into the water from a boat. The net was weighted with lead around its edges, and as it sank, it surrounded the fish. Jesus called his first disciples while he was walking along the lakeshore. "Simon, who is called Peter" (v. 18) was named first among those Jesus called. Peter's prominence will be reinforced by the attention the Gospel gives to this leading figure among the disciples. Peter and his brother Andrew were casting a net, and the other pair of brothers, James and John, was mending their nets when Jesus called them to follow him.

Jesus's call emphasizes that his disciples will share in his mission. The metaphor of fishing for people reflects the seaside location of the calling. If Jesus had called farmers, perhaps he would have challenged them to plant the seed of the gospel; if fellow carpenters, he may have invited them to build the community of faith. Fishing for men and women is not something these fishermen were already equipped to do. Jesus will make them into fishers of people as they learn to follow in his way and as their lives are transformed in the process. The New Testament will show how Peter spread the net of the gospel broadly, drawing many into the kingdom.

It seems that several characteristics of good fishermen are also important qualities for good disciples. The patience and perseverance required for fishing must mark the life of disciples because of the frequent discouragement and hardship they encounter. The sense that those who fish have for the right moment to drop the net is the kind of sensitivity needed by disciples to know the longings and deep needs of people's lives. Those who fish know how to choose the right bait to catch the fish; so, too, disciples must be immersed in the real lives of people in order to share the message of hope and love that Jesus offers them.

If Jesus were going to choose the ideal person to lead his church, where would he look for such a person? We might suppose that person could be found in Jerusalem among the priests of the temple or perhaps among the educated and talented nobles of the city. Yet, the person Jesus called was not found among the religious leaders or noble families of the capital city. Simon Peter was a rugged fisherman, a simple man from the working class of small-town Galilee. Jesus called ordinary people, not people known for their status, wealth, influence, or social standing. Jesus needed people who would give him themselves. It was not the accomplishments of a person that mattered for Jesus but what he could do with them.

The invitation of Jesus, "Follow me" (v. 19), and the immediate response of Simon Peter is a model for the kind of choice and reorientation that discipleship demands. The circumstances in which that choice is made vary greatly with each individual. Many have been nurtured in faith through the privilege of being raised in a Christian home. Many have had to struggle with faith through great opposition and ridicule. Others have come to faith through a transforming experience in their lives that brought them face-to-face with the urgent need for belief. The decision to follow Jesus is never something imposed upon us. It is ultimately a thoughtful and conscious decision to make Jesus the foundation of our lives and to make God's reign the first priority of our lives.

The scene also emphasizes a deeper reality about the call of Jesus to follow. It is Jesus who chooses and summons those whom he wants to be his disciples. Though it was customary in Jewish circles for students to seek out and choose a master to follow, here the initiative belongs to Jesus. So as much as we decide to follow Jesus and make the decision to reorient our lives around him, we acknowledge, if only in retrospect, that the reverse has been true. In all our searching and choosing, we were being sought and chosen. The one we choose is the one who first chose us.

After studying this text and its commentary, answer these questions:

✝ Why did Jesus chose simple, ordinary people to be his first disciples?

✝ In what ways is sharing the Good News with others like fishing?

Meditatio

Try to find ways to personalize this text, realizing that all Scripture is inspired and able to teach God's truth. These questions will help you apply the text to the context of your life.

‡ What does being a fisher of men and women mean in the context of my own life? How is Jesus leading me to be a fisher within his kingdom?

‡ At what point in my life did I begin to see my Christian faith as a personal choice to follow Jesus? Were there any particular events that helped move me from culturally accepted religion to personal discipleship?

‡ How did Jesus desire to transform the net of Peter into the network of God's saving community? What are the similarities between Peter's net and my network of relationships?

Oratio

Pray to God from your heart in whatever way seems to respond to the divine Word spoken to you in the Scriptures. You may use this prayer as a launching pad to continue praying in your own words.

Master Jesus, as with Peter, you know me better than I know myself. You see characteristics and potential within me that I cannot discern. Help me to listen to your call and accept your invitation to follow you. Guide me through your Spirit in the way of discipleship.

Continue to pray the words that arise from your heart . . .

Contemplatio

Imaginatively place yourself in a boat on the sea, on the top of a mountain, or in some other location where you can easily experience the divine presence. Let the words of Jesus, "Come, follow me," echo through your spirit.

After a period of contemplative silence, write a few words about your experience.

Operatio

In what way might you be able to be a fisher of a man or woman today? What could you say or do to gently invite someone into the network of salvation?

2

The Mission of the Twelve

Lectio

*Create a sacred space around you and sanctify this time of lectio by lighting a
candle, ringing a chime, or kissing the page of Scripture as you begin to read.*

MATTHEW 10:1–10

¹Then Jesus summoned his twelve disciples and gave them authority over unclean spirits, to cast them out, and to cure every disease
and every sickness. ²These are the names of the twelve apostles: first,
Simon, also known as Peter, and his brother Andrew; James son of
Zebedee, and his brother John; ³Philip and Bartholomew; Thomas
and Matthew the tax collector; James son of Alphaeus, and Thad-
daeus; ⁴Simon the Cananaean, and Judas Iscariot, the one who betrayed him.

⁵These twelve Jesus sent out with the following instructions: "Go
nowhere among the Gentiles, and enter no town of the Samaritans,
⁶but go rather to the lost sheep of the house of Israel. ⁷As you go,
proclaim the good news, 'The kingdom of heaven has come near.'
⁸Cure the sick, raise the dead, cleanse the lepers, cast out demons.
You received without payment; give without payment. ⁹Take no gold,
or silver, or copper in your belts, ¹⁰no bag for your journey, or two
tunics, or sandals, or a staff; for laborers deserve their food.

Continue to explore the meaning and significance of Peter's mission in the plan of God.

Peter is called both a "disciple" (v. 1) and an "apostle" (v. 2). These two words express the double dimension of Peter's life in relationship to Jesus. A disciple is one who follows and learns from another. An apostle is one who is sent out by another.

After his call to follow Jesus, Peter spent his time with Jesus. He lived with Jesus, listened to him, prayed with him, and accompanied him in his work. Then the time came for Peter to be sent out by Jesus to share in his mission. Peter continued to do what he had learned from Jesus. His mission from Jesus was twofold: to preach and to heal. Through words and deeds, Peter went out to extend to others the Good News he had received.

Jesus had a particular concern for his own Jewish people, to whom God had revealed the covenant. On this first mission, Jesus instructed his apostles to go only to the Jews, the "lost sheep of the house of Israel" (v. 6). Jesus chose the Twelve because they symbolized the twelve tribes of Israel, and it was to gather all of Israel to the kingdom that the Twelve were sent forth. These twelve apostles would eventually represent the foundation of the church, the new Israel, and would be sent out first to the Jewish people and then to the whole world. In this work of restoring and renewing Israel, Jesus was not replacing what God had done among his people in Israel's past but was bringing that work to completion.

Jesus sent out the apostles as a prefiguring of the future work of the church. Their mission was, fundamentally, to continue and prolong the mission of Jesus. They were to preach the gospel and heal the sick, in essence, to say and do what Jesus said and did. The proclamation of the Good News of the kingdom must be accompanied and made believable by signs of the kingdom. These concrete manifestations of the kingdom were not just amazing displays of power but, more importantly, demonstrations of God's care for hurting people. Neither in the ministry of Jesus and his disciples nor in the latter work of the church is there any separation between preaching and healing, between proclaiming the gospel and performing acts of compassion for people in need.

In every list of the Twelve in the Gospels, the name of Peter is first. Matthew also points out that Peter is "first." This is not an adverb indicating that Peter was the first called but an adjective describing Peter himself. Peter ranks first among the Twelve. That he is first indicates his prominent and leading role among the disciples of Jesus and in the early church as the Gospels were being written. Matthew's list calls him "Simon, also known as Peter." Simon, a form of the name Simeon, was a common Jewish name and one of the twelve sons of Jacob the patriarch of Israel. It will be revealed later why Jesus gave Simon the name Peter.

The double agenda of Peter as "disciple" and "apostle" is a model for everyone called by Jesus. As a disciple, Peter cultivated a deep and personal life with Jesus. Sometimes Jesus interacted with his disciples as a whole group; other times it was just Jesus and Peter. Discipleship means developing an individual relationship with Jesus through study, reflection, and prayer with God's Word. It also means cultivating a relationship with other disciples through communal worship, shared prayer, and service to others.

As an apostle, Peter was sent out to preach and heal. Those who follow Jesus and learn from him are then sent out to share with others what they have received. The apostolic work of evangelization means spreading the good news of Jesus through word and deed. Bringing other disciples to Jesus and proclaiming the news of God's kingdom are essential parts of the life of anyone called by Jesus.

After reading the text and commentary, write out your answers to these questions:

‡ Why is it important to be a follower of Jesus before being sent out by him?

‡ In what ways is discipleship both individual and communal? How were both of these dimensions expressed in Peter's relationship with Jesus?

Meditatio

Spend some time reflecting on the implications of the biblical text for your own life, then write out your answers to these questions.

‡ What is the significance of the designation of Peter as "first" among the apostles? How is this adjective manifested in the life of Peter with Jesus and into the early church?

‡ In what ways does the church continue the apostle's mission of preaching and healing today? What could be my role in this double mission of the church?

‡ Why is evangelization only effective when it is a matter of both words and deeds—preaching the kingdom as well as performing signs of the kingdom?

Oratio

Respond to God's Word using the words of this prayer or those of your own.

> Lord Jesus Christ, you called Peter to follow you and you sent him out to continue your mission. As I listen to your Word and imitate your compassion, give me the grace to be your disciple and to extend your work in the world today. Empower me with your Spirit to proclaim God's kingdom in word and deed.

Continue praying with trust and confidence in the Lord, who first called you . . .

Contemplatio

God's intimate knowledge of you is too wonderful to understand. Trust that the One who knows you completely is empowering you from within with the Holy Spirit.

After spending some moments in trusting confidence, write a few words about your experience.

Operatio

In what particular way can I evangelize today in words? How can I also proclaim the gospel with my deeds?

3

Jesus Heals in the House of Peter

Lectio

As you read the Scripture and commentary, highlight or underline passages that seem most pertinent to you. These marks will help you recall your experience of hearing the Scripture and seeking to understand its significance.

MATTHEW 7:24–27; 8:14–17

24"Everyone then who hears these words of mine and acts on them will be like a wise man who built his house on rock. 25The rain fell, the floods came, and the winds blew and beat on that house, but it did not fall, because it had been founded on rock. 26And everyone who hears these words of mine and does not act on them will be like a foolish man who built his house on sand. 27The rain fell, and the floods came, and the winds blew and beat against that house, and it fell—and great was its fall!"

14When Jesus entered Peter's house, he saw his mother-in-law lying in bed with a fever; 15he touched her hand, and the fever left her, and she got up and began to serve him. 16That evening they brought to him many who were possessed with demons; and he cast out the spirits with a word, and cured all who were sick. 17This was to fulfill what had been spoken through the prophet Isaiah, "He took our infirmities and bore our diseases."

Continue searching for the meaning and significance of this text.

Peter's house was in the town of Capernaum on the northwestern shore of the Sea of Galilee. Here Peter lived with his wife and mother-in-law, and the household probably also included children and extended family. Capernaum became the primary base of operations for Jesus's Galilean ministry, and the Gospels indicate that this house of Peter was the place where Jesus stayed. Jesus and his disciples would leave Capernaum on their extended journeys and then return to the village when the missions were complete. Upon their return, Jesus and Peter, and possibly some of the other disciples, would stay at this house, with Peter's wife and mother-in-law offering meals and hospitality for their rest.

No ancient texts prior to the Gospels mention Capernaum, but archaeological excavations have uncovered evidence of first-century dwellings. The town supported a synagogue, and it profited from fishing, as the many fishhooks found there indicate. The remains of a first-century boat were also found nearby, demonstrating the type of small boat used by Galilean fishermen.

Archaeologists have excavated what they identify as the house of Simon Peter in Capernaum. Evidence suggests that it was a simple family home at the time of Jesus. Later in the first century, the walls of this house were plastered, and Christians began carving prayers in the walls, indicating it served as an early house church. The pilgrim Egeria, in the fourth century, wrote in her travel diary, "In Capernaum a house church was made out of the house of Peter, and its walls still stand today." In the fifth century, an octagonal church was built over the site, marking it as a sacred place. Today a modern church with glass floors stands over the site, allowing worshipers to gaze down at the ancient remains.

Houses at the time of Jesus consisted of several rooms clustered around open courtyards. Rooms were dark and sometimes windowless and were used mostly for sleeping and shelter from the weather. Most of life was lived outdoors and in the courtyards extended families shared. The floors and walls of Peter's house and those of his neighbors were made of black volcanic rock called basalt. These sturdy supports held up roofs made of beams or branches covered with mud and thatch. When violent storms came off the lake, the stone houses would stand steady, though the roofs demanded frequent replacement.

The Gospel's mention of the house of Peter (Rock) reminds the careful reader of Jesus's previous reference to a "house on rock" (v. 24). Jesus says that the wise builder uses rock as the foundation of his house. When a house is built on rock, it is able to withstand the onslaught of rain and floods and violent winds. The metaphor suggests the importance of building a life based on the words of Jesus and putting those words into action. These references to the house of Peter and the importance of building a house on rock form the background, then, for the Gospel's later description of Jesus's giving Simon the name Peter, which means rock. He will be the strong foundation on which Jesus will build his church. Because of its solid base, no evil forces will be able to prevail against it (16:18).

This house of Peter is the place where Jesus healed many who were overcome by demons and sickness. Mark's Gospel recounts the dramatic healing of the paralyzed man whose four friends removed part of the roof from Peter's house and lowered the man on his mat to the feet of Jesus (Mark 2:1–4). The healing of Peter's mother-in-law is one of the earliest recorded miracles of Jesus. Since women in those days were often identified by their closest male relative, her identity in relationship to Peter probably indicates that she had no sons and that her husband had died. Her fever is viewed more as the illness than the symptom, and the description of the healing suggests that the fever is an evil power that fled at the touch of Jesus. Both possession and sickness indicate the rule of evil's power that departs under the authority of Jesus.

The fact that Simon Peter had a mother-in-law means that he was married. Though his wife is not mentioned in this passage, Paul indicates in his writings that Peter's wife accompanied him in his missionary travels during the period of the early church (1 Cor. 9:5). Though she too remains nameless, her service must have been significant, both during the life of Jesus, when her house became the headquarters for Jesus's ministry in Galilee, and also decades later when she and her husband traveled to proclaim the gospel to distant lands. Although Peter gave up his occupation in order to follow Jesus and later to administer the church, there is no indication that he renounced his family ties. The man who built his household on a firm foundation will also prove to be a solid base on which Jesus can build his church.

Meditatio

Picture Peter's house in your imagination. Let the ancient text interact with your own world of memories, ideas, fears, and hopes.

‡ What is the lesson in Jesus's saying about the wise man and the foolish man? How might Peter and the other disciples have interpreted this image?

‡ What is the reminder for me in Jesus's instructions about the importance of building on rock? What is its message for my home life, my marriage, or my ministry?

‡ Imagine what Peter's wife and mother-in-law would have learned about Jesus while living and serving in the house that became the home base for the ministry of Jesus. What might be some memories they shared later in their lives?

Oratio

Pray for your home and family in response to the words you have heard in Scripture.

Healing Jesus, you had no home to call your own, yet you chose a family man to be your first apostle. Bless my home and all those I love. Help me to understand how to integrate my family and domestic life with the challenges of following you.

Continue praying with trusting confidence . . .

Contemplatio

Imagine you are in Peter's house with Jesus and his disciples. Relax with him and feel his presence.

After spending time in this contemplative state, write a few words about your experience.

Operatio

What can I say or do today to create a stronger foundation for my home and domestic life?

4

Faith and Doubt on Troubled Waters

Lectio

Read these familiar words of the Gospel as if for the first time. Let God give you the grace of new insights as you approach the text without preconceived ideas and expectations.

MATTHEW 14:22–33

²²Immediately he made the disciples get into the boat and go on ahead to the other side, while he dismissed the crowds. ²³And after he had dismissed the crowds, he went up the mountain by himself to pray. When evening came, he was there alone, ²⁴but by this time the boat, battered by the waves, was far from the land, for the wind was against them. ²⁵And early in the morning he came walking toward them on the sea. ²⁶But when the disciples saw him walking on the sea, they were terrified, saying, "It is a ghost!" And they cried out in fear. ²⁷But immediately Jesus spoke to them and said, "Take heart, it is I; do not be afraid."

²⁸Peter answered him, "Lord, if it is you, command me to come to you on the water." ²⁹He said, "Come." So Peter got out of the boat, started walking on the water, and came toward Jesus. ³⁰But when he noticed the strong wind, he became frightened, and beginning to sink, he cried out, "Lord, save me!" ³¹Jesus immediately reached out his

hand and caught him, saying to him, "You of little faith, why did you doubt?" ³²When they got into the boat, the wind ceased. ³³And those in the boat worshiped him, saying, "Truly you are the Son of God."

Continue searching for the meaning and significance of this text.

After spending the night alone on the mountain in prayer, Jesus comes walking across the water of the sea toward his disciples' boat as it tosses in the wind and the waves. Amid the howling wind and the labored breath of the rowers, the disciples see a singular physical presence shrouded in darkness moving toward them. Terrified and imagining it is a ghost, the disciples cry out in fear. Jesus immediately reassures them that he is there to rescue them from the peril of the sea.

The scene is both a revelation of Jesus's divine nature and a manifestation of his power to save. The Old Testament abounds in texts of divine rescue from storm as well as manifestations of divine power over the sea. Jesus's words, "It is I" (v. 27) are literally translated "I Am," the self-designation of God throughout the Hebrew Scriptures. The divine name, accompanied by the divine command, "Do not be afraid," frequently expresses God's desire to save his people from danger.

Peter asks to share in Jesus's power to walk upon the sea, and he is invited by Jesus to do so. Peter's audacious request is not intended as a demonstration of power alone but harmonizes with his call to discipleship. Jesus had commanded Peter to follow him and had given his disciples a share in his own redemptive mission. Peter desires to follow in Jesus's steps and to take part in his sovereign mission to rescue those in peril. So at the invitation of Jesus, "Peter got out of the boat, started walking on the water, and came toward Jesus" (v. 29).

The scene shows us both faith and doubt. Peter walks on the troubled waters as he depends on Jesus, as he trusts him and lets him take charge. Yet, Peter begins to sink when the wind and the waves begin to overwhelm him, as he takes his focus off Jesus. Peter cries out, "Lord, save me!" (v. 30) and the hand of Jesus is immediately there to hold him up. How far had Peter walked on the water before he began to fail? How deep had he sunk before Jesus reached out his hand? Matthew's Gospel is not concerned with such details. The important reality is that Peter stepped out in faith and walked on the sea and that Jesus rescued him when Peter was overcome with fear.

The life of Peter with Jesus is a continual pattern of invitation, risk, failure, and rescue. Peter teaches us that the best disciples are not those who always succeed. Peter needed to sink in order to take the next step of faith in Jesus. The best learning in discipleship is accomplished through failure. When we fail while attempting great things, even when our failure is caused by doubt and fear, we are growing in faith. Faith is not a possession but an activity. It is like a song that disappears when we stop singing. Jesus urges us to grow, to reach, to dare, and to know that no matter what happens, he will be there with us.

The scene challenges us to be open to what seems impossible: walking on water, feeding thousands with a few loaves, rising from the dead, forgiving an enemy, giving precious time to prayer, giving away hard-earned money, standing alone for what is right and just. All these seem impossible to fulfill, but at the invitation of Jesus, we can step out in faith and attempt the impossible. When we keep our focus on Jesus, we begin to live in the new world of the kingdom.

We can be sure we are living in that new world of the seemingly impossible when, like the half-soaked Peter and the other disciples in the boat, we worship Jesus and proclaim him as the Son of God (v. 33). Worshiping Jesus as Lord always begins with a cry for help, but it is completed in the boat with Jesus as we learn courage and mastery of fear so that we can go forth in faith knowing that Jesus is with us.

After searching for the fuller significance of this Scripture, try to answer these questions:

✢ Why did Peter first seek the invitation of Jesus before he began to walk across the water?

✢ Why did Peter begin to sink?

Meditatio

Spend some time reflecting on the story in relationship to your own life. Let this ancient text interact with your own world of memories, ideas, fears, and hopes. Write out your answers to these questions.

‡ The wavering faith of Peter shows how difficult it is to maintain trusting confidence when we are tossed about in life's surging waves. In what ways does this story reassure me?

‡ In what tone of voice might Jesus have spoken to Peter: "You of little faith, why did you doubt?" Exasperation, concern, gentleness, humor, sadness? Why did Jesus respond to Peter in this way?

‡ When have I attempted to do the impossible? Did I succeed or fail? Did I cry out for help? Did I grow in faith?

Oratio

Respond to your encounter with the Lord in this Scripture in the words of prayer.

Son of God, you called Peter to step out of the boat and walk on the turbulent sea. As I seek to respond to your invitation to grow in faith, help me to reach, risk, and dare to do what seems impossible. Let me know that your saving hand is always there to lift me up.

Continue praying with the confidence of faith . . .

Contemplatio

Imagine Jesus reaching out his hand to you. Place your hand in his and rest in his desire to rescue you. Spend some quiet moments letting Jesus build up your courage and confidence.

After your time of silent contemplation, write a few words about your experience.

Operatio

How is Jesus inviting me to grow in faith today? To what risk is he challenging me as he calls me to step out in faith?

5

The Rock Foundation of Christ's Church

Lectio

Kiss the sacred text of Scripture as a sign of honor to God's Word within it.
Ask the Holy Spirit to guide your listening and understanding.

MATTHEW 16:13–20

[13]Now when Jesus came into the district of Caesarea Philippi, he asked his disciples, "Who do people say that the Son of Man is?" [14]And they said, "Some say John the Baptist, but others Elijah, and still others Jeremiah or one of the prophets." [15]He said to them, "But who do you say that I am?" [16]Simon Peter answered, "You are the Messiah, the Son of the living God." [17]And Jesus answered him, "Blessed are you, Simon son of Jonah! For flesh and blood has not revealed this to you, but my Father in heaven. [18]And I tell you, you are Peter, and on this rock I will build my church, and the gates of Hades will not prevail against it. [19]I will give you the keys of the kingdom of heaven, and whatever you bind on earth will be bound in heaven, and whatever you loose on earth will be loosed in heaven." [20]Then he sternly ordered the disciples not to tell anyone that he was the Messiah.

After carefully reading the Scripture, continue searching for the meaning and significance of the text.

The popular perception of Jesus was that his message bore supernatural authority (v. 14), but Jesus's primary concern was the understanding of his own disciples (v. 15). "Who do you say that I am?" is a question that not only challenged the original disciples but also challenges all people of faith. Everyone who encounters the person of Jesus through the ages must respond to this central question.

Peter's response indicates that he is no longer just the spokesperson for the disciples but that he speaks on his own behalf. "You are the Messiah, the Son of the living God" expresses a faith that is not possible through superior human insight but only through God's grace (vv. 16–17). Because Peter has spoken not through human experience but rather through divine revelation, Jesus declares him blessed and assigns him a unique role.

Now that Peter has announced who Jesus is, Jesus declares who Peter is. Jesus gives Simon the new name "Peter," which, in effect, bestows upon him a new identity. In the Old Testament, God gave new names to those who took on major roles at critical times in God's plan for his people. Abram and Sarai became Abraham and Sarah; Jacob became Israel. In the language of Matthew's Gospel, the Greek name *Petros* creates a wordplay with *petra*, the Greek word for rock. In Aramaic, however, the language of Jesus and the early church, the saying is more exact: "You are *kepha*, and on this *kepha* I will build my church" (v. 18). The parallelism makes it clear that Peter himself is the rock, the sturdy foundation upon which Jesus will construct the edifice of his church.

Jesus has already declared that any wise builder constructs his house on rock (7:24–25). With such a solid base, the house will not fall despite the fiercest of storms. Now Jesus announces that he will build his church on the foundation of Peter, "and the gates of Hades will not prevail against it" (v. 18). These gates of the netherworld represent the powers of death and evil. With such a firm foundation, the church will not crumble or fall despite the fiercest of opposition.

When Jesus hands Peter "the keys of the kingdom" (v. 19), he is offering him the means of opening the way to life for countless people. Through

Peter's preaching and leadership within the church, he will lead people into God's kingdom. A similar image occurs in Isaiah, where a certain Eliakim is made master of the household and given "the key of the house of David" with the authority to open and shut the gates for those seeking entry into the palace (Isa. 22:22). As keeper of the keys, Peter is made the master of Jesus's household, with the privilege of welcoming people into the church. The authority to "bind" and "loose" can refer to admitting or excluding from the community, imposing rules and sanctions, or interpreting and applying the teachings of Jesus for the church.

This scene projects a future for Peter that extends beyond the Gospel. His service as the rocky foundation and his ministry of the keys will continue into the life of the early church. As authoritative leader within the community, Peter will receive revelations and make decisions about the church's life and practices that will have far-reaching consequences. Yet, Peter's role in the church is only in union with the other disciples and in the service of Jesus his Lord, who says at the end of the Gospel, "I am with you always, to the end of the age" (28:19).

After reading the Scripture and commentary, answer these questions to build your understanding:

‡ Why does Jesus say that Simon Peter is "blessed"?

‡ What is the significance of giving Simon a new name with his new role?

‡ What are some of the possible meanings of the authoritative symbol of the keys?

Meditatio

Reflect on the character of Peter and the charge he receives from Jesus. Consider the implications of his role in the life of the church.

‡ Jesus says that Peter's profession of faith in Jesus is a result of divine grace rather than human insight. In what sense is my belief in Jesus more a result of God's revelation than my human reason?

‡ Why do people in the Bible receive a new name when given a new mission? In what sense is Peter's new name an indication of his mission among God's people?

‡ What does Jesus's assurance that the church will prevail over all the powers that oppose it mean to me?

Oratio

Son of the living God, you give your disciples the grace to understand your mission and you call them to roles of service in your church. Deepen my faith in you and strengthen my commitment to serve your church. Help me to trust that your church will endure through opposition and that you are with us forever.

Continue praying for the gift of deeper faith . . .

Contemplatio

Trust that Christ's church has a firm foundation and that the powers of evil will not prevail against it. Be still and rest in that trust while the powers of evil batter its gates.

After your time of quiet stillness, write a brief note about your experience of contemplation.

Operatio

What is my role in Christ's church? What can I do to open its gates for others?

6

The Rock Becomes a
Stumbling Block

Lectio

Ask the Holy Spirit to guide your reading so that you grow to understand the message and inspired truth that God wishes you to understand from this text. Listen carefully with the ears of your heart.

MATTHEW 16:21–28

²¹From that time on, Jesus began to show his disciples that he must go to Jerusalem and undergo great suffering at the hands of the elders and chief priests and scribes, and be killed, and on the third day be raised. ²²And Peter took him aside and began to rebuke him, saying, "God forbid it, Lord! This must never happen to you." ²³But he turned and said to Peter, "Get behind me, Satan! You are a stumbling block to me; for you are setting your mind not on divine things but on human things."

²⁴Then Jesus told his disciples, "If any want to become my followers, let them deny themselves and take up their cross and follow me. ²⁵For those who want to save their life will lose it, and those who lose their life for my sake will find it. ²⁶For what will it profit them if they gain the whole world but forfeit their life? Or what will they give in return for their life? ²⁷For the Son of Man is to come with his angels in the

glory of his Father, and then he will repay everyone for what has been done. ²⁸Truly I tell you, there are some standing here who will not taste death before they see the Son of Man coming in his kingdom."

After carefully reading this Gospel text, continue exploring its significance for the life and ministry of Peter.

Immediately after Peter proclaims Jesus to be the Messiah, the Son of God, and Jesus establishes Peter as the rock of the church, Jesus begins to explain more deeply the meaning of his own life. "From that time on" (v. 21) Jesus turns from teaching and healing the crowds and begins to prepare his disciples for his cross and his death. Jesus explains that it is not his mission to be a powerful, conquering Messiah or a glorious, regal Son of God. There is no other way than the way of the cross. Suffering and death will be the inevitable results of his life of self-giving and love. Discipleship means following a humble, Suffering Servant who will die an ignoble death.

This is too much for the impulsive Peter, and he takes Jesus aside and begins to argue with him. How can the long-awaited king, the great hope of Israel, come to such a disgraceful end? Peter's response, "God forbid it, Lord! This must never happen to you," shows how far Peter is from understanding the implications of Jesus's mission (v. 22). Peter thinks he understands better than Jesus what it means for Jesus to be the Messiah and Son of God. His retort is no doubt motivated by love for Jesus and probably some fear for his own life. If Jesus was going to be put to death, what might this mean for those who follow him?

Jesus's response to Peter contains some of the harshest words recorded from Jesus's mouth (v. 23). He calls Peter "Satan," a tempter. Peter is trying to deflect Jesus from the path that God has set before him. Peter is tempting Jesus to take the easy way out, to give in to selfish desires for security and glory. Jesus replies, calling Peter an obstacle, "a stumbling block," in his path. The rock of the church has become an obstruction to Jesus's mission. Yet, Jesus does not tell Peter, "Away with you, Satan," as he had told his tempter in the wilderness (4:10); rather, Jesus tells Peter, "Get behind me, Satan," commanding him to resume his position as a follower, walking behind Jesus in discipleship.

Despite the spotlight that shines on the figure of Peter throughout the Gospel, Matthew refuses to idealize him. He highlights his weaknesses and failures along with his sturdy faith and preeminent role among the disciples. Before Peter can truly follow Jesus, he has to learn the cost of discipleship: "If any want to become my followers, let them deny themselves and take up their cross and follow me" (v. 24). Peter has to learn from Jesus how to replace his self-centered ambition and desire for prestige with recognition of the value of self-sacrifice. He has to learn how to lose himself in Christ, to take his mission, his way of life, and his very identity as his own. Peter has to learn that being a disciple of Jesus means taking up the cross, not grudgingly enduring it but embracing it, being willing to suffer for the gospel, and getting behind Jesus in order to follow in the way that he leads.

Surely Matthew's Gospel intends the lessons of Peter to be lessons that must be learned by the whole church. Like Peter, the community of disciples must learn that it is not enough to confess Jesus as Messiah and Son of God. He must be acknowledged as the suffering and crucified Lord, and this confession must be expressed not only in verbal doctrine but also in practice. The church of Jesus Christ must be a cruciform church, shaped and transformed by the cross. This emphasis of Matthew's Gospel on practical Christianity is underlined by the sayings about the coming judgment: "For the Son of Man is to come with his angels in the glory of his Father, and then he will repay everyone for what has been done" (v. 27). At the final judgment, our lives will be assessed by their conformity to the cross of Jesus.

After listening carefully to the Scripture, write out your answers to these questions:

‡ Why did Peter rebuke Jesus?

‡ What is the meaning of Jesus's admonishment to Peter, "Get behind me, Satan" (v. 23)?

Meditatio

Spend some time reflecting on the Scripture in terms of your own disciple-ship. After meditating on the questions, write out your answers to each.

✣ What does Peter's transformation from rock to stumbling block teach the church? What does Peter's failure teach me for my discipleship?

✣ Self-denial is not simply choosing to give up certain pleasures in life. It is extinguishing self-centeredness and losing myself in the mission of Christ. What are some of the key moments in my growing discovery of the cost of discipleship?

✣ How did Peter gradually come to understand the meaning of Jesus's words, "For those who want to save their life will lose it, and those who lose their life for my sake will find it" (v. 25)? What can Peter teach me about the value of losing my life for Christ so that I can truly find my life?

Oratio

Speak to God in response to the words, ideas, and images from your lectio.
Offer to God what you have discovered in yourself from your meditatio.

> Suffering Servant of God, by denying the necessity of your cross, Peter the Rock became a stumbling block in the way of your saving mission. Teach me how to take up the cross and follow after you. Show me what it means to lose my life so that I may find it.

Continue with a prayer from your own heart . . .

Contemplatio

Spend some time gazing upon the image of a cross. Let that image sink into your mind and begin to mold your heart. Trust that Jesus is transforming your life into a cruciform existence.

After your experience of contemplation, spend a moment writing a few notes about it.

Operatio

Taking up one's cross does not mean passively enduring whatever suffering comes in life. Rather, it refers to the willingness to suffer the consequences of living the gospel. In what way am I being challenged to take up the cross and follow Jesus?

7

Peter Experiences Jesus Transfigured

Lectio

As you read the biblical verses, listen for God's voice within the words of the inspired text.

MATTHEW 17:1–9

¹Six days later, Jesus took with him Peter and James and his brother John and led them up a high mountain, by themselves. ²And he was transfigured before them, and his face shone like the sun, and his clothes became dazzling white. ³Suddenly there appeared to them Moses and Elijah, talking with him. ⁴Then Peter said to Jesus, "Lord, it is good for us to be here; if you wish, I will make three dwellings here, one for you, one for Moses, and one for Elijah." ⁵While he was still speaking, suddenly a bright cloud overshadowed them, and from the cloud a voice said, "This is my Son, the Beloved; with him I am well pleased; listen to him!" ⁶When the disciples heard this, they fell to the ground and were overcome by fear. ⁷But Jesus came and touched them, saying, "Get up and do not be afraid." ⁸And when they looked up, they saw no one except Jesus himself alone. ⁹As they were coming down the mountain, Jesus ordered them, "Tell no one about the vision until after the Son of Man has been raised from the dead."

Continue listening for the meaning and significance of the text through this commentary.

Throughout Scripture, God's people climbed mountains in order to experience a divine manifestation. Moses went up Mount Sinai to encounter the covenant-making God of Israel. Elijah went to that same mountain and heard God's whispering yet transforming voice. Here Jesus ascends a high mountain with Peter, James, and John for a divine manifestation. He offers them a fleeting glimpse and encouraging insight into the fullness of the divine mystery veiled by his humanity.

Jesus describes their encounter on the mountain as a "vision" (v. 9). This does not reduce the event to an interior or psychological experience, since the three disciples are independent witnesses. Rather, describing the encounter as a vision means that it is a God-given experience, a visualization that is beyond the ordinary functioning of human eyes. God grants the disciples the ability to see what otherwise would have been imperceptible to mortal beings. They are caught up in a holy and fascinating vision that they cannot adequately articulate, a mystery that must be contemplated rather than described.

The lives of Moses and Elijah, representing the Torah and the prophets, embody the whole of God's ancient history with Israel. These two central figures of the Old Testament prepared the way for Jesus in the long drama of the world's salvation. Now that divine drama continues in the life of Jesus as he begins his journey to Jerusalem, the way that leads to the cross. The transfiguration, which occurs in the Gospel at the beginning of that way to the cross, is a revelation to Peter, James, and John of the meaning of that saving journey.

Peter's instincts are correct to suggest that he erect three "dwellings" on the spot (v. 4). The word indicates the temporary, makeshift shelters erected during the Jewish Feast of Sukkoth to remember Israel's forty-year journey through the desert. Peter's remembrance of the saving path of Exodus is a reminder that the disciples are still on the way with Jesus. As Moses and Elijah prepared his way, Jesus prepares Peter, James, and John to travel with him to Jerusalem and to continue his way into the early church. Uncertain of where their journey will lead, these disciples will be models of Christian discipleship for future generations.

From Mount Sinai throughout the journey in the wilderness, the cloud was an expression of God's presence overshadowing his people along the way. After confirming that Jesus is who Peter declared him to be, God's voice from the cloud says, "Listen to him." (v. 5). Listening to Jesus means both hearing and obeying what he says. As Peter, James, and John continue the journey with Jesus to Jerusalem, they must keep listening to what Jesus teaches them and live by those teachings. Listening to Jesus is the way to follow in his footsteps—listening to the Word of God that transfigures sinners into forgiven and redeemed people, that transfigures sick and disabled bodies into healed and whole beings, that transfigures bread and wine into his body and blood, that transfigures suffering and death into resurrected life.

Though it would have been easier to stay on the mountain, Jesus touches his disciples and urges them to get up and walk back down the mountain by his side (v. 7). But he also tells them, "Do not be afraid." Peter, who is unable to conceive of Jesus's suffering and being put to death, is enlightened and uplifted through this vision of Jesus's transfigured glory. Yet, Peter has to learn that the moment of glory was not given to him for its own sake; it is to help him seek the presence and the will of God in all things. The vision on the mountain will help him realize that his walk with Jesus to Jerusalem, his own way of the cross, will also be clothed with radiance. Peter teaches all future disciples that there is only one option for a disciple: we must feel the touch of Jesus, look up from our doubt and fear, and stand up to move forward with Jesus.

After considering this encounter with the transfigured Jesus, try to answer these questions:

✝ Why do Moses and Elijah appear with Jesus in this vision of transfiguration?

✝ What is the significance of Peter's suggestion that he make three dwellings?

Meditatio

Spend some time imaginatively placing yourself within this biblical scene, allowing the words and images to interact with your own thoughts, questions, concerns, and ideas as you reflect on these questions:

✝ Why did Jesus show his transfigured glory to his disciples at the beginning of their journey to Jerusalem? What keeps me engaged and motivated along the path of discipleship?

✝ This narrative joins the most important personages of the Old Testament with the most significant figures of the New Testament. What am I learning from this scene about my life in relationship to God?

✝ God tells the disciples to "listen" to Jesus as he teaches them the way of discipleship on the journey toward Jerusalem. As I reflect on God's command to listen to Jesus, what am I being challenged to believe or to do?

Oratio

Respond to God's Word with heartfelt prayer. Let this prayer be an incentive to continue with your own:

Transfigured Lord, I want to stay with you on the mountain, but you call me to descend with you to life's valleys. Help me to see your glory shining through life's difficult moments. Teach me to listen to you so that I may obey and follow in the way you desire for my life.

Continue asking for God's guidance . . .

Contemplatio

Imaginatively place yourself on the mountain with Jesus. Feel his transfigured presence, and let the voice of God, "Listen to him," resonate within you. Spend some time in the quiet majesty of this moment.

After giving yourself some contemplative space, write a few words about your experience.

Operatio

As Peter prayerfully reflected on the words and deeds of Jesus, Jesus was gradually but surely transfiguring him into a greater expression of the mystery of Christ. In what way do I sense myself being transformed through lectio divina into the presence of Christ for others?

8

Peter Questions
the Limits of Forgiveness

Lectio

*Read aloud the words of this text so that you not only read them with your
eyes but also hear them with your ears. Listen carefully to these inspired words.*

MATTHEW 18:21–35

²¹Then Peter came and said to him, "Lord, if another member of
the church sins against me, how often should I forgive? As many as
seven times?" ²²Jesus said to him, "Not seven times, but, I tell you,
seventy-seven times.

²³"For this reason the kingdom of heaven may be compared to a
king who wished to settle accounts with his slaves. ²⁴When he began
the reckoning, one who owed him ten thousand talents was brought
to him; ²⁵and, as he could not pay, his lord ordered him to be sold,
together with his wife and children and all his possessions, and payment to be made. ²⁶So the slave fell on his knees before him, saying,
'Have patience with me, and I will pay you everything.' ²⁷And out
of pity for him, the lord of that slave released him and forgave him
the debt. ²⁸But that same slave, as he went out, came upon one of
his fellow slaves who owed him a hundred denarii; and seizing him
by the throat, he said, 'Pay what you owe.' ²⁹Then his fellow slave

fell down and pleaded with him, 'Have patience with me, and I will pay you.' [30]But he refused; then he went and threw him into prison until he would pay the debt. [31]When his fellow slaves saw what had happened, they were greatly distressed, and they went and reported to their lord all that had taken place. [32]Then his lord summoned him and said to him, 'You wicked slave! I forgave you all that debt because you pleaded with me. [33]Should you not have had mercy on your fellow slave, as I had mercy on you?' [34]And in anger his lord handed him over to be tortured until he would pay his entire debt. [35]So my heavenly Father will also do to every one of you, if you do not forgive your brother or sister from your heart.'"

After allowing the inspired text to penetrate your mind and heart, continue listening to the text through this commentary:

This scene is set within an extended discourse of Matthew's Gospel in which Jesus offers instructions to his church. Addressed to Peter and the other leading disciples, Jesus's words teach the leaders about the importance of being humble like children, of practicing pastoral care for vulnerable members of the community, of carefully handling disputes and wayward members, and of exercising unlimited forgiveness. The discourse illustrates these teachings with the parable of the lost sheep, emphasizing that church leaders should do everything possible so that none may be lost, and with this parable, stressing God's boundless graciousness toward sinful humanity.

In this section of the discourse, Peter poses to Jesus a hypothetical case about a fellow disciple who wrongs him over and over again. He wants to know when he can draw the line and stop forgiving. Will forgiving the same offense seven times be enough? Peter assumes he is being generous by suggesting seven times as a reasonable limit. Surely after the third or fourth wrong we may assume that the offender is not going to change and doesn't deserve more forgiveness.

The answer of Jesus, "Not seven times, but, I tell you, seventy-seven times" (v. 22), exhorts unlimited forgiveness. Jesus's response alludes to the response of Lamech, a descendent of Cain, who boasts that he will exact overwhelming vengeance on anyone who dares to attack him: "If Cain is avenged sevenfold, truly Lamech seventy-sevenfold" (Gen. 4:24).

Jesus presents forgiveness as the polar opposite of revenge. Disciples must renounce the instinct to retaliate against someone who repeatedly wrongs them.

The impact of this parable of Jesus is found first in the contrast between the huge debt owed by the slave, a massive amount that could never possibly be repaid, and the rather small debt owed to the slave. The parable's effect is found next in the contrast between the king's deeply emotional and bighearted decision to forgive the slave's debt completely and that same slave's brutal and merciless response to his fellow slave. Because the slave had already been forgiven an astounding and unpayable obligation by his king, he should have lived his life in memory of that amazing grace.

This illustration of Jesus's teaching shows us that we must be constant in our forgiving because God's forgiving mercy toward us knows no bounds. Each of us is that slave who owed a staggering amount but whose debt was pardoned by the merciful king. If such a debt has been forgiven for us by God, how generous should we be in forgiving others? Peter's question addressed a human problem from a human perspective. This parable of the kingdom grounds forgiveness in the very nature of God.

Jesus urges disciples to "forgive your brother or sister from your heart" (v. 35). Although we have been lovingly forgiven by our God, we can only open our lives to receive that forgiveness when we forgive others from our hearts. As we forgive one another, we allow the tremendous forgiveness of God to take hold of our lives and renew us from within. God's forgiveness then overflows from our lives into Christ's church.

Now that you have read the text and comments carefully, answer these questions:

‡ What does Peter's question indicate about his character?

‡ What is the meaning of Jesus's instructions to forgive seventy-seven times?

Meditatio

Imagine how Peter would have responded to Jesus's teaching and the emotions involved in this encounter. Consider the significance of this teaching for your own discipleship.

✝ How does it feel to be forgiven? Why is experiencing forgiveness important for psychological health and wholeness?

✝ In what way does Jesus desire his church to be an instrument of forgiveness? How can I be a better channel of God's forgiveness?

✝ Do we forgive others so that God will forgive us, or does God forgive us so that we will be forgiving people? How does God's amazing gift of forgiveness penetrate our hearts?

Oratio

After considering Jesus's teaching in terms of your own life experiences, respond to God's Word with the words that rise from your heart.

> Our Father, forgive us our trespasses as we forgive those who trespass against us. Make me a channel of your healing mercy and lead your church to be an instrument of your forgiveness in the world today. May we forgive our brothers and sisters from the heart.

Continue praying in whatever words express the content of your heart . . .

Contemplatio

Kneel or bow before God, who is your true and only king. Spend some moments contemplating the undeserved forgiveness your king has extended to you. Ask God to give you a forgiving heart.

Following your contemplative experience, write a few words describing it.

Operatio

What steps can I take to forgive someone from the past who has wronged or injured me?

9

The Challenges and Rewards of Discipleship

Lectio

Prepare to read the Scripture by asking God's Spirit to open your mind, your lips, and your heart so that you may hear God's Word within this text.

MATTHEW 19:23–30

²³Then Jesus said to his disciples, "Truly I tell you, it will be hard for a rich person to enter the kingdom of heaven. ²⁴Again I tell you, it is easier for a camel to go through the eye of a needle than for someone who is rich to enter the kingdom of God." ²⁵When the disciples heard this, they were greatly astounded and said, "Then who can be saved?" ²⁶But Jesus looked at them and said, "For mortals it is impossible, but for God all things are possible."

²⁷Then Peter said in reply, "Look, we have left everything and followed you. What then will we have?" ²⁸Jesus said to them, "Truly I tell you, at the renewal of all things, when the Son of Man is seated on the throne of his glory, you who have followed me will also sit on twelve thrones, judging the twelve tribes of Israel. ²⁹And everyone who has left houses or brothers or sisters or father or mother or children or fields, for my name's sake, will receive a hundredfold, and will inherit eternal life. ³⁰But many who are first will be last, and the last will be first."

After a careful reading, continue listening for the significance and message of this passage through these remarks:

Peter's personality is impulsive, straightforward, and often blunt. His question to Jesus seems most inappropriate at this point (v. 27). In effect Peter is asking, "After giving up so much for you, what are we going to get out of it?" Jesus could have scolded Peter and told him that he had missed the point of discipleship once again. Yet, Jesus uses Peter's demanding inquiry to teach him. The purpose of following Jesus is not to earn a reward but to open oneself to the fullness of life that God offers.

In describing the difficult obstacle that riches pose for those who seek entry into God's kingdom, Jesus uses an unforgettable hyperbole (v. 24). The camel was the largest animal in Palestine, and the eye of a needle was the smallest opening in a familiar object. Jesus is telling his disciples that the attraction of wealth and possessions is so alluring that a rich person, with his or her own might, is unable to sever its grasp. Just as it is impossible for a camel to crawl though a needle's eye, depending on riches, privilege, and security creates an insurmountable obstacle to sharing in the kingdom.

Israel's prophets had taught how yearning for wealth can lead to the exploitation of the poor, neglect of one's covenant obligations, and a divided heart. The words of Jesus are set within this prophetic teaching on the corrosive power of wealth. Yet, when the disciples heard this maxim of Jesus, "they were greatly astounded" (v. 25). They apparently assumed that wealth is a sign of God's favor. If those who enjoy God's favor find it so difficult to enter God's kingdom, then how can anyone enter God's kingdom?

The heart of Jesus's teaching, for Peter and all the disciples, lies in the response of Jesus to the question "Then who can be saved?" (v. 25). His answer implies that it is impossible from a human standpoint to overcome the powerful lure of wealth and to be dependent on God alone. The process of being saved, the transformation that takes place as a person enters eternal life, is impossible for human beings to achieve on their own, "but for God all things are possible" (v. 26). Just as God gave us our mortal life as a gift, God can save us from sin and death and give us eternal life.

Salvation cannot be earned by a person. No amount of good works, sacrifice, and self-denial can ever merit salvation for anyone. Salvation is given to us out of the merciful love of God. By doing God's will and following in the way of Jesus, we rid ourselves of all the obstacles that stand in the way of God's saving initiative. By joining our own sacrificial deeds and self-giving actions to the sacrifice of Christ, we cooperate with God's salvation and open our lives to the grace God offers us through faith.

Peter's question is a natural one: "Look, we have left everything and followed you. What then will we have?" (v. 27). If it is impossible for human beings to save themselves, have we given up everything for nothing? Would we be just as well off if we were still fishing? Are our human efforts pointless? Jesus assures Peter that their commitment to Jesus is not in vain and that the Twelve will have glorious roles in the age to come. As Jewish literature foresees, the twelve tribes of Israel will be regathered and renewed in the age of the Messiah. Jesus tells the Twelve that they will rule over this renewed people of God that Jesus is establishing. Even though now they seem to have given up everything, their losses will be made up many times over, and they will experience the fullness of life forever. Even though now they seem poor and persecuted, seeming to be the "last" in the eyes of the world, they will be "first" as they share in God's glory.

After reading the Scripture and commentary, answer these questions to help focus your thoughts:

✝ What is the main point in Jesus's proverb about riches (v. 24)?

✝ In light of Jesus's teachings, who will be "first" and who will be "last"?

Meditatio

As you spend some time reflecting on this episode, try to personalize God's message by allowing this passage to resonate with your own challenges and hopes.

‡ Why were Peter and the other disciples so astounded by the teachings of Jesus on wealth? Why is it so difficult for the rich to enter God's kingdom?

‡ Today many people enjoy the securities, privileges, and comforts that only the very wealthy enjoyed at the time of Jesus. How do I grapple with Jesus's warning about the dangers of riches?

‡ Jesus says that those who leave family and property for his sake will receive a hundredfold. What does this mean in light of Peter's wife, family, and house in Capernaum? What have I given up or left behind to follow Jesus?

Oratio

Speak these words of prayer in response to your reflection on Jesus's teachings to Peter and the other disciples.

> Lord Jesus, you invite me to follow you and to detach myself from the lure of temporal security, worldly influence, and material wealth. Give me the security of your grace, the influence of your Spirit, and the riches of your kingdom.

Continue praying, using the words that come to you after meditating on this passage . . .

Contemplatio

Spend a few moments in silence, asking God's Spirit to work within you, freeing you from the lure of riches and self-sufficiency. Slowly repeat the words of Jesus, "For God all things are possible."

Spend a few moments writing about your contemplative prayer.

Operatio

What do I need to relinquish or leave behind in order to deepen my commitment to Jesus?

10

Jesus Foretells
Peter's Denial

Lectio

Read the passage slowly and carefully. As you read the Scripture and commentary, note any words or phrases that strike you personally.

MATTHEW 26:31–35

³¹Then Jesus said to them, "You will all become deserters because of me this night; for it is written,

'I will strike the shepherd,
and the sheep of the flock will be scattered.'

³²But after I am raised up, I will go ahead of you to Galilee." ³³Peter said to him, "Though all become deserters because of you, I will never desert you." ³⁴Jesus said to him, "Truly I tell you, this very night, before the cock crows, you will deny me three times." ³⁵Peter said to him, "Even though I must die with you, I will not deny you." And so said all the disciples.

Try to discern the deeper significance and meaning of this text through the commentary that follows.

Though Matthew's Gospel highlights the unique role of Peter among the disciples, the Gospel text does not hesitate to show both the strengths of Peter and his tragic weaknesses and failures. The same Peter who professes the truth of Jesus's identity and is called to be the foundation of the church is also called a tempter and a stumbling block by Jesus. Peter's faith allows him to walk on the turbulent waters, but he is overcome with doubt and fear. Peter, who leaves all to follow Jesus and witnesses his transfigured glory, also underestimates the necessity of forgiveness and seeks a reward for his efforts. We are shown the flaws in Peter's character—the chips in the Rock—but we are also shown, through the Gospel's praise and criticism of Peter, how God is working through the life of this great disciple.

One of Peter's chief troubles as a disciple is his inability to accept the cross of Jesus. Peter refuses to believe the reality of the cross and its implications for his own life. The cross is the stumbling block that causes Peter and many halfhearted followers to fall away. Indeed, Jesus predicts that during the night of his betrayal and arrest, all his disciples will run away and leave him alone (v. 31).

The failure of the disciples is described through a citation of the prophet Zechariah. Jesus identifies himself as "the shepherd." When he is struck down, the sheep of his flock will be scattered. Though Jesus had defined discipleship as taking up the cross and following him (16:24), when the test comes, all will desert him. Yet, Jesus adds a hint of a hopeful future to this dismal scene: "But after I am raised up, I will go ahead of you to Galilee" (v. 32). The scattered disciples will be gathered together by the risen Jesus, and once again in Galilee, Jesus will lead them like a shepherd leading his flock. Though they will abandon him that night, in faithful love he will restore them to discipleship.

Peter refuses to consider the possibility of his own failure: "Though all become deserters because of you, I will never desert you" (v. 33). Though Peter allows that Jesus might be right about all the others, Peter is certain that his own faith will never be shaken. Peter is convinced that his commitment is stronger than that of the others, that his discipleship can overcome all obstacles. This is the arrogant self-confidence of a man bound for failure. Peter's overconfidence in his own abilities and his lack of humble reliance on God leave him unprepared for the crisis he will face. Jesus knows Peter's weaknesses, yet he still allows him to fail. Jesus obviously loves Peter, but he does not remove the challenges that face him. The passion of Jesus becomes the point of crisis for Peter. The contrast between the words of Peter and those of Jesus could not be sharper. Peter says to Jesus, "I will never desert you" (v. 33), and increasing his bravado, "I will not deny you" (v. 35). Never? Jesus responds to the presumptuousness of Peter by stating that Peter will abandon him that very night, that he will deny him, in fact, three times. As Peter affirms his undying loyalty to Jesus, he sets himself up for failure. He will demonstrate how fragile his commitment really is when the trying challenge comes.

The irony of this narrative becomes apparent in the scenes that follow: as Peter sleeps rather than prays with Jesus, as he flees at the arrest of Jesus, and as he swears with an oath that he does not know Jesus. Peter's bluster holds a lesson for all future disciples. We may be willing, but we are weak. We may be completely sincere in our commitment to follow Jesus, but because that confidence is rooted in our own ego, we may not have the strength to carry it out. If we do not recognize our vulnerability, then we have set ourselves up for failure. Rather than trust ourselves never to fail, it is better to place our confidence in a power beyond our own, to put our trust in Jesus, who promises to restore us with faithful love when we fail.

After considering the meaning and implications of this narrative for disciple-ship, answer these questions:

‡ In what way does Jesus show his disciples that he is the true shepherd?

‡ In what way does the text emphasize the irony of Peter's brazen certainty that he will never forsake Jesus?

Meditatio

Reflect on this dialogue between Jesus and Peter. Think about what God might be teaching you through their interaction.

‡ Why was Peter so overconfident in his discipleship? How could he be so convinced of his own strength? Why was he unprepared for the crisis?

‡ When have I denied or betrayed my discipleship? In what way was I restored?

‡ Why did Jesus allow Peter to fail? Why does God allow me to fail?

Oratio

Humble your heart before God and ask God to strengthen your discipleship.

Good Shepherd, you have called me to follow you, but I depend on the presence of your Spirit for my strength. Help me prepare for testing and crisis by recognizing my weakness and trusting in your faithful love.

Continue praying for the desire to follow the Shepherd . . .

Contemplatio

In quiet and stillness, spend time allowing God to work within your heart. Ask for the grace of discipleship to prepare you for the crises to come.

Write a few words about this experience of contemplative prayer.

Operatio

What have I learned from my past failures? How can I use my learning to prepare for the future?

11

Jesus Urges Peter
to Watch and Pray

Lectio

Close off the distractions around you and enter a moment of stillness.
Breathe in, being filled with the presence of God's Spirit. Breathe out, letting
go of all that could distract you from this sacred time.

MATTHEW 26:36–46

³⁶Then Jesus went with them to a place called Gethsemane; and he said to his disciples, "Sit here while I go over there and pray." ³⁷He took with him Peter and the two sons of Zebedee, and began to be grieved and agitated. ³⁸Then he said to them, "I am deeply grieved, even to death; remain here, and stay awake with me." ³⁹And going a little farther, he threw himself on the ground and prayed, "My Father, if it is possible, let this cup pass from me; yet not what I want but what you want." ⁴⁰Then he came to the disciples and found them sleeping; and he said to Peter, "So, could you not stay awake with me one hour? ⁴¹Stay awake and pray that you may not come into the time of trial; the spirit indeed is willing, but the flesh is weak." ⁴²Again he went away for the second time and prayed, "My Father, if this cannot pass unless I drink it, your will be done." ⁴³Again he came and found them sleeping, for their eyes were heavy. ⁴⁴So leaving

them again, he went away and prayed for the third time, saying the same words. ⁴⁵Then he came to the disciples and said to them, "Are you still sleeping and taking your rest? See, the hour is at hand, and the Son of Man is betrayed into the hands of sinners. ⁴⁶Get up, let us be going. See, my betrayer is at hand."

Continue listening for God's Word as you further explore the meaning and significance of the inspired text.

As Jesus arrives at Gethsemane with his disciples, he knows full well that Peter's pledge of faithful discipleship and loyalty in crisis will be shown as well-intentioned but empty chatter. Jesus departs from the larger group of disciples in order to pray, taking with him only Peter and the two sons of Zebedee. The scene demonstrates the fullness of Jesus's humanity. He is "grieved and agitated" (v. 37), distressed, anguished, fearful, and worried, needing the supportive companionship of his dearest friends as he prepares for his pending arrest. He urges his three closest disciples to remain near him and stay awake.

These are the same three disciples Jesus invited to be with him at the transfiguration. As Jesus had taken Peter, James, and John away to a high mountain to reveal his glory to them alone, now Jesus takes the same inner group of disciples out of the crowded city to a quiet garden on the Mount of Olives. In both scenes, Jesus takes the three disciples aside from the others to reveal the depth of his mission. As they had witnessed Jesus in glory, they now see him in weakness and anguish as he faces impending death. If they are to understand Jesus, they must understand his suffering as well as his glory.

The prayer of Jesus at Gethsemane is the most intimate portrait the Gospels offer of Jesus at prayer. In this quiet place, Jesus "threw himself on the ground" (v. 39) and began to pray in anguish. This prostrate position with his face to the ground is a stance of complete submission and respect. The content of the prayer is similar in many respects to the prayer Jesus taught his disciples (6:9–13). Jesus addresses "my Father" (v. 39), and he prays "your will be done" (v. 42). Simultaneously, Jesus begs for deliverance, "let this cup pass from me" (v. 39), and for a resolute commitment to God's will, a poignant paradox that is typical of honest prayer from the heart in times of crisis. Jesus knows that suffering and death lay ahead of him, yet he also knows that he must go on. The cup of suffering, the abandonment of friends, the way of the cross—these are the challenges that test the limits of Jesus's trust and acceptance.

The fervent prayer of Jesus is strongly contrasted with the disciples' behavior. When Jesus returns the first time to find his disciples sleeping, he scolds Peter directly. Jesus says to Peter, "So, could you not stay awake with me one hour? Stay awake and pray that you may not come into the time of trial" (vv. 40–41). Even after this explicit imperative, Jesus returns in bitter disappointment to find his disciples sleeping a second time. The cycle then repeats itself a third time, right up to the moment of Jesus's betrayal and arrest. This sequence in which Peter fails to stay awake and pray anticipates Peter's three denials of Jesus still to come.

Jesus's insistence to Peter that the disciples "stay awake and pray" (v. 41) is far more than a request to be vigilant at that moment. Praying not to come into "the time of trial" is another connection to the Lord's Prayer. Prayerful anticipation and readiness for the challenges to come must be the constant stance and attitude of followers of Jesus. Despite Jesus's warning, Peter does not prepare himself through prayer for his time of trial. Because the disciples are not spiritually vigilant, they are unprepared for the overwhelming crisis of Jesus's passion.

Peter's deepest struggle lies not in his physical fatigue but in the unresolved struggle between "the spirit" and "the flesh" (v. 41). The spirit inclines us to serve God; the flesh, in its boastful independence from God, is intent on serving itself. In the time of trial, Jesus reveals the victory of the spirit over the flesh, while the disciples exhibited the victory of the flesh over the spirit. Only with vigilance and prayer can this conflict be resolved in favor of single-minded fidelity to God.

Following your reading of the Scripture and commentary, answer these questions:

‡ In what ways is Jesus shown to be fully human in this narrative?

‡ In what ways is Jesus's prayer at Gethsemane similar to the Lord's Prayer that he taught his disciples?

Meditatio

Use your imagination and enter the scene yourself. Reflect on these questions from the viewpoint of your own life to understand the text's fuller meaning:

✦ How could Jesus have experienced such radiance in God's presence at the transfiguration and here experience such anguish? Why was it necessary that Peter experience Jesus as both glorious and agonized if he was going to grow as a disciple?

✦ Why do I experience deep joy when I feel God close to me only to be followed later by anguish when God seems so far away? Why are both experiences necessary for the development of my relationship to God in prayer?

✦ What can I learn about prayer from this account? What is the one thing I don't want to forget?

Oratio

Pray with the words of Jesus in the garden and with the words that spring from your own relationship with God.

My Father, teach me to desire only what you desire and to do your will in all things. Help me to pray and keep me connected to your presence. Keep me vigilant and incline my spirit toward you so that when trials come I will be ready to face whatever life brings.

Continue to pray from the heart . . .

Contemplatio

Imaginatively place yourself in the Garden of Gethsemane with Jesus. Feel the emotions of the moment. Spend some quiet time in watchful vigilance with Jesus.

Write a few words about your imaginative experience of contemplative prayer.

Operatio

How can I grow more watchful through prayer? What commitment can I make to stay awake and pray?

12

Peter Denies Knowing Jesus before the Cock Crows

Prepare to listen to the Word of God in Scripture. Slowly speak the words of the sacred text aloud. Read the text with your eyes and hear it with your ears.

MATTHEW 26:57–58, 69–75

[57]Those who had arrested Jesus took him to Caiaphas the high priest, in whose house the scribes and the elders had gathered. [58]But Peter was following him at a distance, as far as the courtyard of the high priest; and going inside, he sat with the guards in order to see how this would end.

[69]Now Peter was sitting outside in the courtyard. A servant-girl came to him and said, "You also were with Jesus the Galilean." [70]But he denied it before all of them, saying, "I do not know what you are talking about." [71]When he went out to the porch, another servant-girl saw him, and she said to the bystanders, "This man was with Jesus of Nazareth." [72]Again he denied it with an oath, "I do not know the man." [73]After a little while the bystanders came up and said to Peter, "Certainly you are also one of them, for your accent betrays you."

[74]Then he began to curse, and he swore an oath, "I do not know the man!" At that moment the cock crowed. [75]Then Peter remembered what Jesus had said: "Before the cock crows, you will deny me three times." And he went out and wept bitterly.

After listening with imagination to this inspired text, continue to search for its significance.

The reason for Peter's denial of Jesus was suggested in the previous scene in which Jesus urged Peter to "stay awake and pray that you may not come into the time of trial" (v. 41). Where Jesus prayed three times, Peter slept three times. The result of Peter's failure to be vigilant in prayer is his three refusals to acknowledge Jesus.

This narrative of Peter surrounds the scene of Jesus's interrogation before the high priest's council (vv. 59–68). In this way, the Gospel suggests that the two scenes are occurring simultaneously. As Jesus is confronted by verbal threats from the high priest and remains steadfast, Peter is tested by servants and cowers in fear and denial. He is accused of being "with Jesus" (vv. 69, 71). The same phrase is used in other scenes to indicate the intimate bond that exists between Jesus and his disciples. It is his belonging to Jesus, a relationship built up and enriched through many experiences, that Peter denies in his weakness.

The drama builds in intensity as the threefold denial gradually escalates to a powerful climax. First, Peter denies "before all of them" that he even knows what the servant-girl is talking about (v. 70). Then, questioned by another servant-girl, he explicitly declares with an oath that he does not know Jesus (v. 72). Finally, when the bystanders come over to accuse him, Peter begins to curse, and he swears with an oath, "I do not know the man!" (v. 74). As the drama is mounting, Peter is gradually retreating: at first he is "sitting outside in the courtyard" (v. 69), then he moves "out to the porch" (v. 71), and finally he flees the scene after realizing the horror of what he has done.

Perhaps we should not be too harsh on Peter, remembering that he was the only one of the Twelve who remained; all the others fled. Peter was torn between fear that made him want to run away and courage that made him want to stay in the courtyard near Jesus. The rooster's crow, piercing the darkness of those early hours, made Peter realize the tragedy of his denial. Peter's love for Jesus remained, however. His response to his failure made all the difference in whether his personal failure would lead to defeat or to triumph. Unlike Judas, whose response to his betrayal led him to the despair of suicide, it was that undying love that made Peter remember Jesus's words, weep with remorse, and repent.

Peter's denial is reported with minor variations in all four Gospels. The story must have been told by Peter and others as a striking illustration of the triumph of grace over human weakness. In the context of the persecuted church to which the Gospels were written, Peter's story stood as a sign of hope for the many early Christians who denied knowing Jesus in the crisis of persecution or betrayed their discipleship under threat. Many had renounced their faith under oath in order to save the lives of their families and had wept the same bitter tears of remorse. In telling the story of Peter, the evangelists earnestly wanted these Christians to know that even the greatest Christian leader had failed in his discipleship at the critical hour. Through their failure, they could, like Peter, discover the deeper meaning of the cross, the power of the resurrection, and Christ's forgiving grace.

After listening for God's Word in the Scriptures, answer these questions about the text:

✝ In what way does the evangelist show Peter moving from evasion to perjury to cursing in order to disassociate himself from Jesus?

✝ Why was this embarrassing narrative included in all four of the Gospels?

Meditatio

Think about the ways this passage speaks to your struggles with faithful discipleship. Reflect on these questions in order to understand the text's personal message for you:

‡ Have I ever been afraid to admit that I am a disciple of Jesus? What was the source of my fear?

‡ What has been the "crowing rooster" in my life that helped me realize a failure or flaw in my discipleship?

‡ The story of Peter's denials has helped struggling Christians through the ages. What do Peter's denials teach me?

Oratio

Express your prayer to God in union with the remorseful and repentant Peter.

Gracious God, Peter did not desire to betray Jesus; he just wasn't strong enough not to. Help me to realize that my sincerity and good-will are not enough to keep me from failing you. Strengthen my weaknesses and continue to look upon me with your merciful love.

Continue to express the words that arise from your heart to God . . .

Contemplatio

Place yourself in the presence of Jesus. Realize that you have denied him in many ways, yet he loves you anyway, despite your failures. Rest in his healing and forgiving grace.

Write a few words about this contemplative experience.

Operatio

The experience of love when we don't deserve it is the grace that offers us healing and self-confidence. How can I show someone that kind of love today?

13

Peter Refuses
to Leave Jesus

Lectio

In a comfortable and quiet place, read the Scripture carefully, asking God's Spirit to guide you in your understanding.

JOHN 6:52–69

52The Jews then disputed among themselves, saying, "How can this man give us his flesh to eat?" 53So Jesus said to them, "Very truly, I tell you, unless you eat the flesh of the Son of Man and drink his blood, you have no life in you. 54Those who eat my flesh and drink my blood have eternal life, and I will raise them up on the last day; 55for my flesh is true food and my blood is true drink. 56Those who eat my flesh and drink my blood abide in me, and I in them. 57Just as the living Father sent me, and I live because of the Father, so whoever eats me will live because of me. 58This is the bread that came down from heaven, not like that which your ancestors ate, and they died. But the one who eats this bread will live forever." 59He said these things while he was teaching in the synagogue at Capernaum.

60When many of his disciples heard it, they said, "This teaching is difficult; who can accept it?" 61But Jesus, being aware that his disciples were complaining about it, said to them, "Does this offend you? 62Then what if you were to see the Son of Man ascending to where he was before? ⁶³It is the spirit that gives life; the flesh is useless. The words that I have spoken to you are spirit and life. ⁶⁴But among you there are some who do not believe." For Jesus knew from the first who were the ones that did not believe, and who was the one that would betray him. ⁶⁵And he said, "For this reason I have told you that no one can come to me unless it is granted by the Father."

⁶⁶Because of this many of his disciples turned back and no longer went about with him. ⁶⁷So Jesus asked the twelve, "Do you also wish to go away?" ⁶⁸Simon Peter answered him, "Lord, to whom can we go? You have the words of eternal life. ⁶⁹We have come to believe and know that you are the Holy One of God."

Continue seeking the deeper meaning and significance of this passage by considering the church's tradition and scholarship.

In John's Gospel, a true disciple of Jesus is one who believes in him, follows him, and, most especially, remains with him. Throughout the narratives, many come to believe in Jesus and follow him for a time, but only those who continue to follow him, remaining through the struggles of discipleship over the long haul, are truly his disciples. Hearing the words of Jesus and seeing his wondrous deeds lead many to believe in him, yet such undeveloped faith is often unsure and tentative. Jesus invites such believers to genuine discipleship, saying, "If you continue in my word, you are truly my disciples" (8:31). The word "continue" may also be translated as "remain" or "abide." Since the teachings of Jesus cannot be embraced quickly or easily, Jesus encourages these emergent believers to live with his Word so that his revelation will gradually change the direction and mission of their lives. Believers will truly be disciples as they abide in the Word of Jesus, creating space for his Word and living with that Word so that it transforms their lives.

The graphic imagery of Jesus's discourse, eating his flesh and drinking his blood, suggests that disciples must be nourished and sustained by Jesus. Genuine disciples must assimilate Jesus as they would food and drink, allowing his life-giving presence to become the very fiber of their being. Jesus insists by stating negatively (v. 53) and positively (v. 54) that whoever consumes his flesh and blood has eternal life now and will be raised up on the last day. In this way, his disciples will "abide" in him and he in them (v. 56).

The eucharistic language of Jesus's discourse evokes the practice of the church to which the Gospel is addressed. The lifting up of Jesus on the cross is the moment of his total self-gift for the life of the world, when his body is broken and his blood poured out. The eucharistic memorial of his saving death and resurrection offers that life in each generation as disciples give thanks for his eternal gift and as they eat his flesh and drink his blood.

Up until now, Jesus's ministry had been successful and well received. Here was the turning point in John's presentation of the Gospel. Many of those who had been following Jesus "turned back and no longer went about with him" (v. 66). They found his teachings difficult and offensive because they did not conform to their human expectations. The only ones who are able to accept the teachings of Jesus are those who are granted the gift of the Spirit and are drawn to Jesus by the Father.

Seeing his followers leaving him, Jesus asks the Twelve, "Do you also wish to go away?" (v. 67). Peter answers as spokesman for the others. His confession of faith affirms that Jesus is the only one to whom they can go, that he alone has the words of eternal life. They have come to believe that Jesus is "the Holy One of God" (v. 68), and, though they do not completely understand his teachings, they trust him enough to know that their understanding will grow as they remain with him and abide in his Word through the struggles of genuine discipleship.

After reading the Scripture and explanatory commentary, consider these questions:

✢ What is the ultimate characteristic of a true disciple according to John's Gospel?

✢ What is the difference between the response of most of Jesus's followers and that of Peter?

Meditatio

Reflect on the meaning of this discourse of Jesus and on the response of Peter. Meditate on their deeper meaning and significance for your discipleship.

‡ What are some of the many layers of meaning included in Jesus's exhortation to eat his flesh and drink his blood?

‡ Why did many of Jesus's disciples find his teaching so difficult to accept (v. 60)? Why did they turn away and cease being his disciples?

‡ In what way is Peter shown to be a model of true discipleship in his response to Jesus?

Oratio

Speak to Jesus in response to the words, ideas, and images from the reading. Use these or similar words:

Holy One of God, I believe that you have the words of everlasting life. Thank you for the gift of your flesh and blood, given for our eternal life. Give me the gift of your Spirit so that I can persevere in following you.

Continue praying in response to your call to lasting discipleship . . .

Contemplatio

Though you do not fully understand the teachings of Jesus, trust in his Word and deepen your desire to abide in him. Slowly repeat the words of Peter, "You have the words of eternal life" (v. 68).

Write a few words about your desire to remain steadfast in Jesus.

Operatio

What can I do to develop my tentative and immature faith? What can I do today to prepare for the long haul of Christian discipleship?

14

Jesus Washes
the Feet of Peter

Lectio

Breathe in, being filled with the presence of God's Spirit. Breathe out, letting go of all that could distract you from this sacred time. Begin reading when you feel ready to hear God's voice.

JOHN 13:3–15

And during supper ³Jesus, knowing that the Father had given all things into his hands, and that he had come from God and was going to God, ⁴got up from the table, took off his outer robe, and tied a towel around himself. ⁵Then he poured water into a basin and began to wash the disciples' feet and to wipe them with the towel that was tied around him. ⁶He came to Simon Peter, who said to him, "Lord, are you going to wash my feet?" ⁷Jesus answered, "You do not know now what I am doing, but later you will understand." ⁸Peter said to him, "You will never wash my feet." Jesus answered, "Unless I wash you, you have no share with me." ⁹Simon Peter said to him, "Lord, not my feet only but also my hands and my head!" ¹⁰Jesus said to him, "One who has bathed does not need to wash, except for the feet, but is entirely clean. And you are clean, though not all of you."

[11]For he knew who was to betray him; for this reason he said, "Not all of you are clean."

[12]After he had washed their feet, had put on his robe, and had returned to the table, he said to them, "Do you know what I have done to you? [13]You call me Teacher and Lord—and you are right, for that is what I am. [14]So if I, your Lord and Teacher, have washed your feet, you also ought to wash one another's feet. [15]For I have set you an example, that you also should do as I have done to you."

After reading this narrative, consider these remarks in order to explore the deeper significance of this encounter between Jesus and Peter.

The unpaved roads of Palestine got extremely dusty in dry weather and awfully muddy when it rained. Sandals gave little protection for the feet of travelers, so the servant of the house was always ready with a towel and washbowl to wash the feet of guests as they arrived. By taking the role of the servant, Jesus shocked his disciples with his humility and gave them a lesson they would not soon forget. In fact, this simple gesture of Jesus has been memorialized by Christians through the ages as a prophetic demonstration of a disciple's lifestyle.

Jesus's entire life was one of self-sacrificing love. As Jesus shares his last supper with his disciples, he shows them what his life has been about and what his death will mean. Jesus is the Servant who gives his life for others out of love. The next day on the cross, Jesus will culminate the work of his entire life.

Peter strongly resists Jesus's action: "You will never wash my feet" (v. 8). Again we see Peter's independence and self-sufficiency rise to the surface. It is difficult for the self-reliant Peter to be served by another. Yet, Jesus plainly states that being a disciple means not only serving others but also learning how to be served by others. Peter has to learn to depend on others, to realize his need to be helped, before he can be a true servant like Jesus.

Jesus's actions reject human relationships characterized by domination. Jesus instead models relationships rooted in self-giving and interdependent ministry. He responds to Peter's resistance by saying, "Unless I wash you, you have no share with me" (v. 8). In other words, unless Peter allows Jesus to wash his feet, Peter cannot be his disciple. The key to the identity and mission of disciples is expressed in the act of foot washing, that is, sharing in the self-giving love that will bring Jesus's life to an end.

The impulsive Peter then urges Jesus to wash not only his feet but his whole body. Jesus's response is a reference to the once-only cleansing involved in Christian baptism. The total washing happens only once, as followers are baptized into the death of Jesus. Foot washing is a partial and limited service that must be constantly repeated. So, too, Jesus gave himself only once on the cross, yet his smaller acts of sacrificial love are repeated frequently through his disciples.

"Do you know what I have done to you?" Jesus asks (v. 12). Do we understand what Jesus has done? Jesus calls his symbolic action "an example," an action that his disciples must imitate for others (v. 15). Because the action of Jesus is an example, it can be expressed by disciples through deeds of compassion, material help to those in need, forgiveness of offenses, and a host of other actions that display sacrificial love for others.

The foot washing foreshadows the self-giving involved in Jesus's death on the cross. The Teacher who washes the feet of his disciples corresponds to the Good Shepherd who lays down his life for his sheep. Later in John's Gospel, Peter will be commissioned by Jesus to care for the sheep of the risen Christ. Following the example of Jesus, Peter will shepherd the flock of his Lord, even to the point of laying down his own life for them.

After truly listening to this moving account of Jesus, write your response to these questions:

⁜ Why did Peter, at first, refuse to let Jesus wash his feet?

⁜ How did Peter learn from the action of Jesus in a way that he couldn't have learned in words?

Meditatio

By meditating on this Gospel scene, consider the significance of this "example" of Jesus for your own discipleship.

✝ Which is more difficult for me: to wash the feet of another or to have my feet washed by another? Why? Why are both necessary?

✝ Why does John's Gospel narrate Jesus's act of washing the feet of his disciples at the Last Supper rather than the institution of the Eucharist, as in the Gospels of Matthew, Mark, and Luke?

✝ How do I answer the question of Jesus: "Do you know what I have done to you?" (v. 12)?

Oratio

Pray to God from a heart that has been changed through your reflection on this scene.

> Faithful Servant, teach me how to accept your service and receive your love. Only by first accepting your grace can I, in turn, express loving service for others. Help me to imitate your self-giving love as your disciple.

Continue praying for the grace to love and serve . . .

Contemplatio

Contemplate this scene by imagining that Jesus is washing your feet. Feel his love for you and be aware of your emotional response. Remain in quiet awe and gratitude.

Write a few words describing this contemplative experience.

Operatio

Jesus said to his disciples, "You also should do as I have done to you." How can I imitate the example of Jesus in the lives of others today?

15

Peter Responds
to the Arrest of Jesus

Lectio

*Close off the distractions of the day and enter a still moment. Read this text
aloud so that you hear the words and listen to the inspired passage.*

JOHN 18:10–27

[10]Then Simon Peter, who had a sword, drew it, struck the high
priest's slave, and cut off his right ear. The slave's name was Malchus.
[11]Jesus said to Peter, "Put your sword back into its sheath. Am I not
to drink the cup that the Father has given me?"

[12]So the soldiers, their officer, and the Jewish police arrested Jesus
and bound him. [13]First they took him to Annas, who was the father-
in-law of Caiaphas, the high priest that year. [14]Caiaphas was the one
who had advised the Jews that it was better to have one person die
for the people.

[15]Simon Peter and another disciple followed Jesus. Since that
disciple was known to the high priest, he went with Jesus into the
courtyard of the high priest, [16]but Peter was standing outside at the
gate. So the other disciple, who was known to the high priest, went
out, spoke to the woman who guarded the gate, and brought Peter
in. [17]The woman said to Peter, "You are not also one of this man's

disciples, are you?" He said, "I am not." [18]Now the slaves and the police had made a charcoal fire because it was cold, and they were standing around it and warming themselves. Peter also was standing with them and warming himself.

[19]Then the high priest questioned Jesus about his disciples and about his teaching. [20]Jesus answered, "I have spoken openly to the world; I have always taught in synagogues and in the temple, where all the Jews come together. I have said nothing in secret. [21]Why do you ask me? Ask those who heard what I said to them; they know what I said." [22]When he had said this, one of the police standing nearby struck Jesus on the face, saying, "Is that how you answer the high priest?" [23]Jesus answered, "If I have spoken wrongly, testify to the wrong. But if I have spoken rightly, why do you strike me?" [24]Then Annas sent him bound to Caiaphas the high priest.

[25]Now Simon Peter was standing and warming himself. They asked him, "You are not also one of his disciples, are you?" He denied it and said, "I am not." [26]One of the slaves of the high priest, a relative of the man whose ear Peter had cut off, asked, "Did I not see you in the garden with him?" [27]Again Peter denied it, and at that moment the cock crowed.

Continue searching for the meaning and significance of this narrative.

In John's account of the arrest of Jesus in the garden, he emphasizes the dramatic contrast between Peter and Jesus. In an attempt to save Jesus from being seized, Peter resorts to armaments and slashes the ear of Malchus with his sword. But Jesus knows that salvation does not lie in the power of weapons but in doing the will of the Father. In contrast to Peter's violent response, Jesus courageously submits to his captors, knowing that he must drink the cup of suffering (v. 11).

The contrast continues after Jesus's arrest. While Jesus is being interrogated by the high priests, Peter is undergoing his own interrogation. When asked whether he is a disciple of Jesus, Peter's consistent answer is, "I am not" (vv. 17, 25). Peter's "I am not" is a sharp contrast to Jesus's consistent response throughout John's Gospel, "I Am." During his trial, Jesus is confident and forthright, while Peter begins to fall apart and fail miserably. Jesus speaks the truth openly to his accusers; Peter denies the truth about himself.

The Gospel juxtaposes the trial of Jesus with this scene of Peter because it is clear that Peter is on trial too. Peter stands near the place where Jesus is being interrogated, warming himself by "a charcoal fire" (v. 18; see also v. 25). That warm fire offers little comfort for Peter as he stands in the darkness of his own fear and self-doubt. Notice that Peter does not deny Jesus's identity. He does not take back his profession of faith in Jesus as the Holy One of God. Peter does not deny Jesus; he denies himself. "I am not," he insists. In his threefold self-denial, Peter refuses to admit the deepest truth about himself.

All human sins and failures are like Peter's denial. They represent a denial of who we are made to be. Yet, with repentance comes forgiveness. Peter is going to recover from his self-defeat, and because of the way he will respond to his collapse, his failure will become the seed of his success. Just as Jesus's death would be the most discouraging news imaginable without the resurrection, Peter's story would be extremely disheartening without his renewal. Peter's rise from defeat to victory is the subject of the remainder of this study.

After listening to this dramatic contrast between Peter and Jesus, respond to these questions:

‡ How does the Gospel writer dramatize the contrast between the witness of Jesus and the denials of Peter?

‡ Why are Peter's denials and the startling cockcrow so important as to be narrated in all four of the Gospels?

Allow this narrative to interact with your own experiences of fear, denial, betrayal, and hope. Repeat and ponder whatever words or phrases strike you from your reading.

‡ What might have been going through the mind of Peter as he stood warming himself by the charcoal fire?

‡ When we sin it is not so much that we break a set of rules as that we deny who we truly are. We betray the truth of who we are made to be. In what way does Peter teach me this truth?

‡ The crow of the rooster marked the end of Peter's denials and the beginning of his courageous lifelong discipleship. How can absolute failure sometimes mark an awakening to triumphant living?

Oratio

Respond to this narrative in the words of prayer. Include whatever words and feelings have arisen within you during your reading and reflection.

> Master Jesus, in my strengths and weaknesses I desire to follow you. I know that you understand me better than I understand myself. May the cockcrow of my conscience stir me to greater discipleship so that I find my truest identity in following you.

Continue voicing the prayer that issues from your heart . . .

Contemplatio

Look upon the cross of Jesus and consider his sacrificial love. Rest in gratitude for his saving gift and for calling you to be his disciple.

Write a few words about your experience of gratitude for Jesus's gift of himself.

Operatio

Jesus helped the impulsive Peter have a better understanding of his own strengths and weaknesses. How can I gain a better sense of my own capabilities and vulnerabilities as a disciple?

16

Discovery of the
Empty Tomb of Jesus

Lectio

Read the passage slowly and carefully, trying not to impose your preconceived understanding on the text. Ask God's Spirit to help you read this familiar passage anew.

JOHN 20:1–10

¹Early on the first day of the week, while it was still dark, Mary Magdalene came to the tomb and saw that the stone had been removed from the tomb. ²So she ran and went to Simon Peter and the other disciple, the one whom Jesus loved, and said to them, "They have taken the Lord out of the tomb, and we do not know where they have laid him." ³Then Peter and the other disciple set out and went toward the tomb. ⁴The two were running together, but the other disciple outran Peter and reached the tomb first. ⁵He bent down to look in and saw the linen wrappings lying there, but he did not go in. ⁶Then Simon Peter came, following him, and went into the tomb. He saw the linen wrappings lying there, ⁷and the cloth that had been on Jesus's head, not lying with the linen wrappings but rolled up in a place by itself. ⁸Then the other disciple, who reached the tomb first, also went in, and he saw and believed; ⁹for as yet they did not

understand the scripture, that he must rise from the dead. [10]Then the disciples returned to their homes.

Continue seeking the meaning and significance of this text through the following comments.

Peter's previous scene in John's Gospel ended in the high priest's courtyard as the stark cockcrow pierced the early morning darkness. We are left wondering how Peter escaped, where he fled, and how he carried on after the dreadful day of Jesus's crucifixion and death. Now the Sabbath has passed, and we see Peter again in the predawn darkness of "the first day of the week" (v. 1). He is awakened by the familiar voice of Mary Magdalene telling him that the body of Jesus has been removed from the tomb. Roman troops, religious leaders, grave robbers—someone must have rolled back the stone and carried off his corpse.

Peter and the other disciple, the one particularly beloved by Jesus, run toward the tomb. When they arrive, the sun has begun to rise, and the disciples can see the linen wrappings of Jesus lying on the stone where the body of Jesus had been. When Peter enters the tomb, he sees not only the strips of linen that had wrapped the body but also the cloth that had covered the face of Jesus rolled up and lying to the side. When the beloved disciple enters the tomb, he intuits the significance of the burial wrappings: "he saw and believed" (v. 8). This does not imply that Peter saw but failed to believe. The beloved disciple is the eye-witness of the Gospel, and the narrative rests on his testimony and is told from his perspective. The beloved disciple is the model for all other disciples to imitate, the one who gathers the evidence and comes to believe that Jesus is indeed risen.

This careful placement of the grave clothes is the disciples' first compelling clue that something exceedingly significant has happened. It convinces them that the body of Jesus has not been stolen, as Mary Magdalene had at first assumed. If the corpse had been taken from the tomb, surely the robbers would not have engaged in the useless task of undressing the body. The arrangement of the linen wrappings and the head cloth lying where the body of Jesus had been laid suggest that an unprecedented divine action has occurred.

The scene at the empty tomb forms a strong contrast to the earlier scene of Lazarus emerging from the tomb. The text says that, at the command of Jesus, "the dead man came out, his hands and feet bound with strips of cloth, and his face wrapped in a cloth" (11:44). The raising of Lazarus was a resuscitation of his body, raised again to temporal life, to a physical life that would continue to age. Eventually he would again die and be buried in a tomb. The resurrection of Jesus was a qualitatively different event. He is risen to new life, to an existence beyond the bounds of space and time, to an eternal life that will never end. The body of Jesus is totally transformed, in a way that the evangelist struggles to describe and that we cannot completely comprehend.

The narrative demonstrates that Peter and the beloved disciple are surprised at what they see and cannot grasp the reality of Jesus's resurrection. The text concludes, "As yet they did not understand the scripture, that he must rise from the dead" (v. 9). Later, with the light of the Holy Spirit, the disciples will read the ancient Scriptures and understand the full plan of God. This is the task of the church in every age: to continually read the Old and New Testaments and understand the dying and rising of Jesus as the culmination of God's saving plan.

Answer these questions after carefully reading this resurrection narrative:

‡ Why does the scene begin in the darkness and continue through the rising dawn?

‡ Why does Mary Magdalene report to Peter that the body of Jesus has been taken from the tomb?

Meditatio

After listening to the text and placing yourself in the scene, consider what you can learn from Peter's experience at the tomb of Jesus on the new day of creation.

✝ According to Genesis 1, God began creation on the first day of the week. In what way is "the first day of the week" in John's narrative the beginning of God's new creation?

✝ What led the disciples who saw the empty tomb to believe that Jesus had been resurrected? In what way is the resurrection of Jesus different from the resuscitation of a corpse?

✝ What hints from the Old Testament lead me to believe that God would not leave Jesus imprisoned in the tomb of death?

Oratio

Consider what you have learned from this passage about the risen Jesus and respond in prayer that reflects your new insights.

> Triumphant Lord, you are the light that shines in the world's darkness and the Savior who cannot be imprisoned in a tomb. Give me the energy to run to you and the insight to know that you are risen to eternal life.

Use the words and images of the text to continue your prayerful response . . .

Contemplatio

Imaginatively place yourself in the empty tomb of Jesus. Trust that he is risen to new life and that your future is full of hope because of his victory over sin and death.

Write a few words summarizing your contemplative experience of Christ's triumph.

Operatio

Those who believe in a joyful future are able to live fuller and richer lives today. In what way does the resurrection of Jesus enable me to experience the beginning of new life coming forth from my present life?

17

Jesus Appears
to Peter at the Sea

Lectio

*Read this scene aloud so that you see the text with your eyes and hear the
words with your ears. Be aware that you are experiencing the Word of God in
the inspired text.*

JOHN 21:1–14

¹After these things Jesus showed himself again to the disciples by
the Sea of Tiberias; and he showed himself in this way. ²Gathered
there together were Simon Peter, Thomas called the Twin, Natha-
nael of Cana in Galilee, the sons of Zebedee, and two others of his
disciples. ³Simon Peter said to them, "I am going fishing." They said
to him, "We will go with you." They went out and got into the boat,
but that night they caught nothing.

⁴Just after daybreak, Jesus stood on the beach; but the disciples
did not know that it was Jesus. ⁵Jesus said to them, "Children, you
have no fish, have you?" They answered him, "No." ⁶He said to them,
"Cast the net to the right side of the boat, and you will find some."
So they cast it, and now they were not able to haul it in because there
were so many fish. ⁷That disciple whom Jesus loved said to Peter, "It

is the Lord!" When Simon Peter heard that it was the Lord, he put on some clothes, for he was naked, and jumped into the sea. [8]But the other disciples came in the boat, dragging the net full of fish, for they were not far from the land, only about a hundred yards off.

[9]When they had gone ashore, they saw a charcoal fire there, with fish on it, and bread. [10]Jesus said to them, "Bring some of the fish that you have just caught." [11]So Simon Peter went aboard and hauled the net ashore, full of large fish, a hundred fifty-three of them; and though there were so many, the net was not torn. [12]Jesus said to them, "Come and have breakfast." Now none of the disciples dared to ask him, "Who are you?" because they knew it was the Lord. [13]Jesus came and took the bread and gave it to them, and did the same with the fish. [14]This was now the third time that Jesus appeared to the disciples after he was raised from the dead.

After listening to this wonderful scene on the sea, continue searching for the full significance and lessons from this passage.

Simon Peter and six other disciples have gathered back in Galilee after the traumatic events of Jerusalem. Characteristically, Peter takes the initiative and declares his intention to go fishing. He is joined by the others, and they all venture out on the sea they know so well. The futility of the disciples' fishing efforts during the night, followed by the tremendous success in the morning light, continue the Gospel's theme of darkness and light. Without Jesus, the disciples catch nothing (v. 3), but with his direction, the catch is overwhelming (v. 6).

With the rising light of dawn, the risen Jesus stands on the shore of the sea, though unrecognized by his disciples. The record-breaking catch is the catalyst to recognition. As in the scene at the tomb, the beloved disciple displays insightful recognition—"It is the Lord"—while Peter exhibits decisive action when "he jumped into the sea" in order to swim ashore to Jesus (v. 7). After the other disciples row the boat to land, it is Peter who hauls the net full of fish ashore (v. 11).

As is characteristic of John's Gospel, this scene can be read on another level. The fishing scene represents the apostolic mission of the church. These fishers of men and women are evangelizing the world and making disciples. Because of the presence and direction of Jesus, their mission is overwhelmingly successful. Jerome, an ancient commentator, suggests that 153 is the number of species of fish known at the time. The net full of 153 large fish represents the universality and all-embracing character of the church's mission. The great catch is the symbolic expression of the great commission Jesus gives his followers at the end of Matthew's Gospel: "Go therefore and make disciples of all nations" (Matt. 28:19). This final resurrection appearance of John's Gospel expresses the image of Peter in the early church, the missionary fisher of people under the direction of the risen Lord.

Jesus has prepared a "charcoal fire" (v. 9) upon which he has placed roasting fish and bread. Though reminding Peter of the charcoal fire outside the high priest's house, these burning coals by the sea prepare a meal of communion and reconciliation. How different this fire must have looked to Peter in the light of dawn as the risen Lord invited the disciples to come and eat.

After carefully listening to the Scripture and commentary, answer these questions:

† In what way does the evangelist use the symbolism of darkness and light in this account?

† In what way is the relationship between Peter and the beloved disciple in this scene similar to their relationship in the scene at the empty tomb?

† How can the net full of fish be read on two levels of meaning?

Meditatio

Read the text again while imaginatively placing yourself within the scene with Peter. Consider your five senses: what you see, hear, smell, taste, and feel.

☩ Describe the sights and sounds, the aromas, the tastes and textures that come alive as you imagine yourself in the scene.

☩ In what ways does Peter show initiative and leadership in this scene? How does the scene express Peter's role as the great fisherman of the church?

☩ What are some of the emotions that Peter must have felt when he saw the charcoal fire that Jesus had prepared on the shore of the sea?

Oratio

As you learn from the mistakes and accomplishments of Peter, express your deepening relationship with Jesus in prayer.

Risen Jesus, give me the insight and faith to recognize your presence today. Bring your light into my darkness, give me confidence in my work, and give me the love to accomplish the mission you give to me this day.

Continue praying in whatever words arise from your loving union with Jesus . . .

Contemplatio

Picture yourself in the warm sunshine on the seashore with Jesus. As he invites you to the meal, let him nourish you with the fish and the bread of his life.

Write a brief note about your feelings during this time of contemplation.

Operatio

In what ways have I experienced the presence and guidance of Jesus making my work successful? How can I better notice his presence and action in my life today?

18

Jesus Calls Peter
to Shepherd His Flock

Lectio

Kiss the words of Scripture, asking God to help you reverence the divine Word within. Be grateful for God's invitation to listen carefully to this Scripture.

JOHN 21:15–19

¹⁵When they had finished breakfast, Jesus said to Simon Peter, "Simon son of John, do you love me more than these?" He said to him, "Yes, Lord; you know that I love you." Jesus said to him, "Feed my lambs." ¹⁶A second time he said to him, "Simon son of John, do you love me?" He said to him, "Yes, Lord; you know that I love you." Jesus said to him, "Tend my sheep." ¹⁷He said to him the third time, "Simon son of John, do you love me?" Peter felt hurt because he said to him the third time, "Do you love me?" And he said to him, "Lord, you know everything; you know that I love you." Jesus said to him, "Feed my sheep. ¹⁸Very truly, I tell you, when you were younger, you used to fasten your own belt and to go wherever you wished. But when you grow old, you will stretch out your hands, and someone else will fasten a belt around you and take you where you do not wish to go." ¹⁹(He said this to indicate the kind of death by which he would glorify God.) After this he said to him, "Follow me."

After listening to this scene with your heart, continue to explore its depths through this commentary.

By making a charcoal fire on the shore, Jesus has, in a sense, re-created the setting in which Peter denied him. The fire reminds Peter of the cold, hostile questioning in the courtyard of the high priest. In the presence of this new fire, which is warm and inviting, Jesus offers Peter another opportunity to affirm his discipleship.

As Peter had three times denied his relationship with Jesus, now Jesus gives Peter this threefold opportunity to express his love for him. Peter responds more cautiously this time, more humbly aware of his vulnerability and limitations. At long last, Peter has learned that he cannot follow Jesus in a way that relies on only his own strength and willpower. Each of his affirmations of love offsets his earlier rejections. In the light of this new day, Peter's agonizing over his denials is brought to an end as he experiences the healing and reconciling presence of the risen Lord.

The question Jesus puts to Peter is ambiguous: "Do you love me more than these?" (v. 15). Is Jesus asking whether Peter loves him more than these fish that they have just caught and eaten, that is, more than his profession? Is he asking if Peter loves him more than he loves these other disciples? Or is Jesus asking whether Peter loves him more than his other disciples love him? All three must be true. Peter must love Jesus more than he loves other people or his fishing business, and he must love Jesus more than the others do because he must be willing to render extraordinary sacrifice on behalf of his master.

Jesus's threefold question leads to his entrusting Peter with the care of his flock. The triple commissioning expresses Peter's solemn obligation. These sheep, so precious to Jesus, are now given to the care of the sinful yet forgiven Peter. This kind of pastoral care is modeled on that of Jesus, the Good Shepherd. The responsibility given to Peter implies total dedication to the community of faith, guidance through teaching and preaching, and self-giving even to the point of giving his life for them.

Jesus had said that the Good Shepherd is willing to lay down his life for his sheep. Jesus follows his commission of Peter as shepherd with a prediction of his death (vv. 18–19). With his freedom taken away, he will be led to the place of execution where he will stretch out his hands in crucifixion. By the time the Gospel was written, the evangelist would have known that Peter died a martyr's death under the persecution of Nero in Rome.

Jesus ends his commissioning of Peter with the same words that began their relationship: "Follow me." Only now Peter's call to follow Jesus takes on a new and deeper meaning. For the remaining decades of his life, Peter will live in the shadow of the cross, just as Jesus did. He will follow the great Shepherd, tending his flock as shepherd of Christ's followers.

Experience shows that those who are forgiven the most are able to love the most. Peter was able to love with fidelity and commitment because he had failed and been forgiven. Stripped of his vain pride and self-reliance, Peter was now able to love Jesus with self-sacrificing love. He was now able to be the rock, the fisherman, the shepherd of the church that Jesus was calling him to be.

After reading the Scripture and commentary, summarize your understanding by answering these questions:

✝ How do the charcoal fire and the three questions of this scene create an experience of déjà vu?

✝ Despite Peter's objections, Jesus asks Peter for a third time, "Do you love me?" (v. 17). Why such insistence on the part of Jesus?

✝ What is the significance for Peter in Jesus's command to be a shepherd?

Meditatio

Allow this encounter of Jesus and Peter to interact with your own experiences of guilt, forgiveness, vocation, and commitment.

✝ Jesus offered the twofold orientation of love and service to heal Peter from his guilt. How do I experience forgiveness of sins and healing from guilt?

✝ Before commissioning Peter for service, Jesus did not ask about his strength or endurance. He asked only if Peter's love for him was supreme. Why does love for Jesus make all the difference?

✝ What is the experience of Peter teaching me about being a disciple of Jesus and serving his church?

Oratio

Pray to Jesus in whatever way seems to respond to the divine Word spoken to you through this text.

> Good Shepherd, you know that I love you. Help me to open my heart fully to you and follow you as a mature and consistent disciple. Help me to love and care for those you have entrusted to me.

Continue praying as the love in your heart directs you . . .

Contemplatio

Place yourself, again, along the seashore with Jesus. Listen to his words to you, "Follow me." Let his words resonate within you and create in you a willing heart.

Write a few words about how Christ is forming your heart for loving service.

Operatio

How is Jesus asking me to follow him today? In what ways am I called to exercise a pastoral service in Christ's church?

19

Peter Addresses
the Crowd at Pentecost

Lectio

*Prepare yourself to listen to Peter's first sermon in the Acts of the Apostles.
Breathe in, being filled with the presence of God's Spirit. Breathe out, letting
go of all that could distract you from this sacred time.*

ACTS 2:12–17, 21–24, 32–41

¹²All were amazed and perplexed, saying to one another, "What
does this mean?" ¹³But others sneered and said, "They are filled with
new wine."

¹⁴But Peter, standing with the eleven, raised his voice and addressed
them, "Men of Judea and all who live in Jerusalem, let this be known
to you, and listen to what I say. ¹⁵Indeed, these are not drunk, as you
suppose, for it is only nine o'clock in the morning. ¹⁶No, this is what
was spoken through the prophet Joel:

¹⁷'In the last days it will be, God declares,
    that I will pour out my Spirit upon all flesh.

²¹Then everyone who calls on the name of the Lord shall be
saved.'

²²"You that are Israelites, listen to what I have to say: Jesus of Nazareth, a man attested to you by God with deeds of power, wonders, and signs that God did through him among you, as you yourselves know—²³this man, handed over to you according to the definite plan and foreknowledge of God, you crucified and killed by the hands of those outside the law. ²⁴But God raised him up, having freed him from death, because it was impossible for him to be held in its power.

³²"This Jesus God raised up, and of that all of us are witnesses. ³³Being therefore exalted at the right hand of God, and having received from the Father the promise of the Holy Spirit, he has poured out this that you both see and hear. ³⁴For David did not ascend into the heavens, but he himself says,

'The Lord said to my Lord,

"Sit at my right hand,

³⁵until I make your enemies your footstool."'

³⁶"Therefore let the entire house of Israel know with certainty that God has made him both Lord and Messiah, this Jesus whom you crucified."

³⁷Now when they heard this, they were cut to the heart and said to Peter and to the other apostles, "Brothers, what should we do?" ³⁸Peter said to them, "Repent, and be baptized every one of you in the name of Jesus Christ so that your sins may be forgiven; and you will receive the gift of the Holy Spirit. ³⁹For the promise is for you, for your children, and for all who are far away, everyone whom the Lord our God calls to him." ⁴⁰And he testified with many other arguments and exhorted them, saying, "Save yourselves from this corrupt generation." ⁴¹So those who welcomed his message were baptized, and that day about three thousand persons were added.

After listening to these words of Peter with the ear of your heart, listen for further understanding as you read the commentary.

The Acts of the Apostles shows Peter in a much more favorable light. His cloud of guilt has been lifted, and he is able to serve with confident enthusiasm. The book will illustrate Peter carrying out the mission entrusted to him by Jesus as fisherman and shepherd of the church. He will fulfill his multiple roles as spokesperson for the apostles, powerful witness to Jesus Christ, and pastoral leader of the church.

At the events of Pentecost, Peter steps forth from the group of disciples and delivers a powerful and courageous sermon. He is confronted by a large crowd; some are mocking antagonists, confusing the effects of the Spirit with inebriation, and others are startled and confused. Probably the crowd includes some who had collaborated in putting Jesus to death. What a change has occurred in Peter since that fateful night he was surrounded by a similarly hostile crowd! The contrast between this bold preaching and Peter's denial of Jesus is ample proof of the power of God working within him.

Peter's discourse explains the events in light of the Scriptures of Israel. The prophet Joel had foretold that the Spirit of God would be poured out on all people. Everyone would have a share in this manifestation of the new age, and the signs around them would proclaim that the age of salvation had come (v. 17). The poetic and apocalyptic language of Joel expresses the radical changes that happen in people's lives as the Spirit of God is given to them.

The heart of Peter's proclamation is the person of Jesus Christ as the fulfillment of Scripture. Peter gives a straightforward presentation of who Jesus is and the significance of his death and resurrection. The heart of Christian witness is the declaration that the crucified Jesus is both "Lord and Messiah" (v. 36).

The preaching of Peter makes a decisive impact on many people and provokes them to ask, "What should we do?" (v. 37). Peter responds with a clear call for a decision involving a no and a yes (v. 38): "Repent," saying no to your past life of rejecting God and living for yourselves, and "Be baptized," saying yes to God by faith in Jesus Christ. Through repentance and baptism, all who enter this new community will receive forgiveness of sins and the gift of the Holy Spirit. Many respond to Peter's exhortation with enthusiastic acceptance, and thousands are added to the community of faith. These form a powerful communal witness to others in the city so that more and more people come to know Jesus as Messiah and Lord.

Meditatio

Consider what this scene of Peter's Pentecost sermon is asking you to learn and remember.

✝ Based upon this sermon at Pentecost, what would I consider to be the heart of the gospel proclaimed by Peter? How would I summarize the Good News of Jesus in one sentence?

✝ In what way is a decision about Jesus both a no and a yes? Why did so many respond enthusiastically to this message?

✝ In what way do I think of myself as a witness to the gospel? How does Peter's witness inspire me to embody the Good News of Jesus?

Oratio

Respond to your God, who knows you intimately, cares about you deeply,
and accepts you unconditionally.

> Messiah and Lord, you continue to call people to repentance and
> baptismal faith through the witness of your disciples. Empower me
> with your Spirit and form me as your witness today. Enkindle your
> church with the fire of the Holy Spirit.

Continue praying with a heart filled with repentance and gratitude for the
gospel...

Contemplatio

Be still and know that the Spirit of God dwells in you. Ask that the gift of the
Holy Spirit be stirred within you. Recognize that you are continually being
created anew through the indwelling Spirit.

Write a few words from your contemplation of God's Spirit.

Operatio

In response to Peter's preaching at Pentecost, what should I do? What is
my no, and what is my yes?

20

Peter Raises
the Lame Man to Walk

Lectio

As you study this text and commentary, highlight or underline the parts you wish to remember and return to for reflection. Let the Holy Spirit guide your careful reading.

ACTS 3:1–16

¹One day Peter and John were going up to the temple at the hour of prayer, at three o'clock in the afternoon. ²And a man lame from birth was being carried in. People would lay him daily at the gate of the temple called the Beautiful Gate so that he could ask for alms from those entering the temple. ³When he saw Peter and John about to go into the temple, he asked them for alms. ⁴Peter looked intently at him, as did John, and said, "Look at us." ⁵And he fixed his attention on them, expecting to receive something from them. ⁶But Peter said, "I have no silver or gold, but what I have I give you; in the name of Jesus Christ of Nazareth, stand up and walk." ⁷And he took him by the right hand and raised him up; and immediately his feet and ankles were made strong. ⁸Jumping up, he stood and began to walk, and he entered the temple with them, walking and leaping and praising God. ⁹All the people saw him walking and praising God, ¹⁰and they recognized him as the one who used to sit and ask for alms at

the Beautiful Gate of the temple; and they were filled with wonder and amazement at what had happened to him.

¹¹While he clung to Peter and John, all the people ran together to them in the portico called Solomon's Portico, utterly astonished. ¹²When Peter saw it, he addressed the people, "You Israelites, why do you wonder at this, or why do you stare at us, as though by our own power or piety we had made him walk? ¹³The God of Abraham, the God of Isaac, and the God of Jacob, the God of our ancestors has glorified his servant Jesus, whom you handed over and rejected in the presence of Pilate, though he had decided to release him. ¹⁴But you rejected the Holy and Righteous One and asked to have a murderer given to you, ¹⁵and you killed the Author of life, whom God raised from the dead. To this we are witnesses. ¹⁶And by faith in his name, his name itself has made this man strong, whom you see and know; and the faith that is through Jesus has given him this perfect health in the presence of all of you."

After reading the inspired text with your mind and heart, continue seeking the Word of the Lord through these comments:

The Acts of the Apostles demonstrates that the ministry of Jesus continues in the apostolic community. The teaching, reconciling, and healing work of the risen Christ is extended into the life of the church through the Holy Spirit of Pentecost. The healing of the crippled beggar points out the parallels between the healings of Jesus in the Gospels and the healings of the apostles. It was as if Jesus were still with them, responding to the needs of the sick and afflicted people who came to him for help.

A man lame since his birth asks for alms at the gate of the temple as he has for years. But on this day, Peter gives him more than money can buy. He gives him the ability to walk. In effect, Peter gives him a new life, which is a portrayal of what salvation does. The miracle is not performed as a feat of magic to amaze the crowds but, like the miracles of Jesus, as a sign of God's saving presence in their midst.

In speaking of the coming salvation of God, the prophet Isaiah had said, "Then the eyes of the blind shall be opened, and the ears of the deaf unstopped; then the lame shall leap like a deer, and the tongue of the speechless sing for joy" (Isa. 35:5–6). The lame man walking, leaping, and praising God is a tangible sign of the wholeness and fullness that salvation brings and that God desires for all people (v. 8).

As he did at Pentecost, Peter uses the opportunity of the crowd's amazement to focus their attention on Jesus Christ. Peter does not heal for his own glory or through his own powers. It is only "in the name of Jesus Christ of Nazareth" (v. 6) that Peter does such miraculous works. He is not in control, manipulating power he has received. Healing, rather, is an expression of faith and a form of prayer that the will of God be done.

Peter directs his speech to his Jewish audience, who knows the Old Testament well. He shows them that Jesus is not just an isolated celebrity but the culmination of a long history of prophecy and expectation. Peter knows that understanding who Jesus is will help them appreciate what Jesus did. He is the Holy and Righteous One who was rejected by those he came to save; in him a tragic human "no" was met by God's wondrous "yes" in the resurrection. The name of Jesus is the direct link between the living Lord in heaven and his church on earth. This name of Jesus is the authority Peter invokes when he preaches; under this name the sick are healed and sins are forgiven. In this name, Jesus is present with his saving power so that Peter can say, "His name itself has made this man strong" (v. 16).

Though the fullness of life is our ultimate destiny, we do not experience it completely in this life. People are broken and wounded, sick and oppressed. Jesus leaves it in the hands of his disciples to be his instruments of healing today. Healing people takes many forms: prayer, medicine, surgery, counseling, forgiveness, and encouragement. Called to heal in the name of Christ, we use whatever means are given to us to enable others to experience healing and fullness of life.

Answer these questions based on your listening to the text of Acts and its commentary:

✝ What has Peter done for the lame man besides enabling him to walk?

✝ In what ways are miracles tangible signs of salvation?

Meditatio

After considering the Scripture and its interpretive commentary, ask yourself what it says and means to you.

‡ What is the difference between miracles and magic? Why was Peter able to work wonders in Jerusalem?

‡ Why did Peter choose to heal this lame man and not others? Why did the author of Acts decide to include this particular healing in his account of the early church?

‡ If we are to be disciples of Christ, our lives and activities must express a healing dimension. In what way am I called to be a healer in the name of Jesus?

Oratio

Express the thoughts and feelings that arise within you after reading this Scripture and address them in prayer to Christ.

> Author of life, I do not have silver or gold, but what I have I want to give. Teach me to be aware of the healing power I possess in the name of Jesus. Help me not to be so busy that I do no good, and motivate me to reach out to suffering people in your name.

Continue pouring out your prayer until words are no longer necessary or useful . . .

Contemplatio

In a quiet and restful place, consider the Spirit of the risen Christ who now dwells within you. Spend these moments cultivating compassion in your heart for hurting people.

Write a few words about your contemplative experience.

Operatio

Every day God places someone in our path who is in need. What kinds of suffering and pain do I encounter most frequently in those around me? What can I do to bring healing to them?

21

Peter Demonstrates the Gospel's Freedom

Lectio

Read this passage aloud so that you will experience the Scripture more fully by seeing it with your eyes, hearing it with your ears, and speaking it with your lips.

ACTS 5:12–32

[12]Now many signs and wonders were done among the people through the apostles. And they were all together in Solomon's Portico. [13]None of the rest dared to join them, but the people held them in high esteem. [14]Yet more than ever believers were added to the Lord, great numbers of both men and women, [15]so that they even carried out the sick into the streets, and laid them on cots and mats, in order that Peter's shadow might fall on some of them as he came by. [16]A great number of people would also gather from the towns around Jerusalem, bringing the sick and those tormented by unclean spirits, and they were all cured.

[17]Then the high priest took action; he and all who were with him (that is, the sect of the Sadducees), being filled with jealousy, [18]arrested the apostles and put them in the public prison. [19]But during the night

an angel of the Lord opened the prison doors, brought them out, and said, [20]"Go, stand in the temple and tell the people the whole message about this life." [21]When they heard this, they entered the temple at daybreak and went on with their teaching.

When the high priest and those with him arrived, they called together the council and the whole body of the elders of Israel, and sent to the prison to have them brought. [22]But when the temple police went there, they did not find them in the prison; so they returned and reported, [23]"We found the prison securely locked and the guards standing at the doors, but when we opened them, we found no one inside." [24]Now when the captain of the temple and the chief priests heard these words, they were perplexed about them, wondering what might be going on. [25]Then someone arrived and announced, "Look, the men whom you put in prison are standing in the temple and teaching the people!"

[26]Then the captain went with the temple police and brought them, but without violence, for they were afraid of being stoned by the people.

[27]When they had brought them, they had them stand before the council. The high priest questioned them, [28]saying, "We gave you strict orders not to teach in this name, yet here you have filled Jerusalem with your teaching and you are determined to bring this man's blood on us." [29]But Peter and the apostles answered, "We must obey God rather than any human authority. [30]The God of our ancestors raised up Jesus, whom you had killed by hanging him on a tree. [31]God exalted him at his right hand as Leader and Savior that he might give repentance to Israel and forgiveness of sins. [32]And we are witnesses to these things, and so is the Holy Spirit whom God has given to those who obey him."

Having listened for God's Word, continue to search for its meaning and message through these comments:

In offering the reader a condensed summary of the work of the infant church, Luke tells us where the apostles met, what happened as a result of their meetings, how others viewed their work, and how the number of followers grew. Solomon's Portico was a covered colonnade on the east side of the temple, a frequent place for rabbis to meet with their disciples and to engage in public teaching. This was the site of some of Jesus's teachings and the place where Peter addressed the crowd after the healing of the lame man. Here the church met openly for all to see. Fear of arrest kept many from joining the apostles, yet their ministry was viewed with high regard by the people (v. 13), and many men and women became believers (v. 14).

The sick were brought out into the streets in the hope of being healed even by Peter's shadow as he passed by. This detail indicates the extent of Christ's power working through him. It is not necessarily the direct touch and awareness of Peter that brought healing to people's lives. Their cures occurred, rather, through faith in Jesus that the presence of Peter inspired within them. Peter had become so transformed through God's Spirit working within him that his closeness conveyed something of the presence of Jesus to people.

This dramatic narrative illustrates how the gospel cannot be contained. The greater the effort made by the authorities to prevent the Good News of Jesus from being proclaimed, the more effective the witness of the apostles becomes. The distinguished Sanhedrin is comically perplexed by the information that, despite all the precautions they have taken, the prisoners are nowhere to be found. Their bafflement is heightened when they are informed that the apostles not only are free but also are preaching again in the temple, the very crime for which they had been arrested and imprisoned.

The impulsive abruptness that characterized Peter in the Gospels has become courageous boldness through the empowerment of the Holy Spirit. Called in before the highest authorities of Jerusalem, he refuses to obey their order to be silent about Jesus. Ordered to cease preaching in the name of Jesus, Peter defiantly responds, "We must obey God rather than any human authority" (v. 29). Standing before them more as their judge than their victim, Peter the fisherman powerfully proclaims the salvation given by Jesus Christ.

The more the apostles were arrested and threatened, the stronger their proclamation became. The persecution of the church in Jerusalem led to the expansion of Christianity into the regions around the city. This seems to be the pattern of the church throughout history. The more it is silenced, oppressed, and persecuted, the more it grows and the stronger it becomes. Truly the gospel cannot be contained.

Meditatio

Reflect on the words of this narrative for your own life. Allow these words to teach you the lesson God wants for you.

✝ Why did Peter refuse to obey the commands of the Jerusalem authorities not to teach in the name of Jesus? What am I learning from Peter's courage?

✝ Why is it impossible to silence and imprison the Good News of Jesus? Why do attempts to contain the gospel usually have the opposite effect?

✝ Through the Holy Spirit, the same power and courage given to Peter is available to us. When have I felt empowered to do something that I felt completely inadequate to do?

Oratio

Respond to God's Word to you with your own words to God. Speak from your heart in response to the insights you have received.

> Lord and Savior, you empowered Peter and the apostles to proclaim the gospel despite opposition and persecution. Release my heart from the imprisonment of fear and make me obedient to the promptings of your Spirit.

Continue to express your struggles and desires in prayer...

Contemplatio

In contemplative silence, ask to be filled with the Holy Spirit. Realize that God is giving you faith, courage, insight, and direction. Receive the spiritual gifts that filled the apostles.

Write a few words about God's gift of the Spirit.

Operatio

When we are living in the Holy Spirit, we are given a desire to say and do things that we might previously have felt were impossible. In what way is God directing me to be a witness to his presence today?

22

Peter Gives New Life
in the Name of Jesus

Read these two healing narratives with thoughtfulness and expectation. Prepare for the new understandings and insight they will offer to you.

ACTS 9:32–42

[32]Now as Peter went here and there among all the believers, he came down also to the saints living in Lydda. [33]There he found a man named Aeneas, who had been bedridden for eight years, for he was paralyzed. [34]Peter said to him, "Aeneas, Jesus Christ heals you; get up and make your bed!" And immediately he got up. [35]And all the residents of Lydda and Sharon saw him and turned to the Lord.

[36]Now in Joppa there was a disciple whose name was Tabitha, which in Greek is Dorcas. She was devoted to good works and acts of charity. [37]At that time she became ill and died. When they had washed her, they laid her in a room upstairs. [38]Since Lydda was near Joppa, the disciples, who heard that Peter was there, sent two men to him with the request, "Please come to us without delay." [39]So Peter got up and went with them; and when he arrived, they took him to the room upstairs. All the widows stood beside him, weeping and showing tunics and other clothing that Dorcas had made while she was with them. [40]Peter put

all of them outside, and then he knelt down and prayed. He turned to the body and said, "Tabitha, get up." Then she opened her eyes, and seeing Peter, she sat up. [41]He gave her his hand and helped her up. Then calling the saints and widows, he showed her to be alive. [42]This became known throughout Joppa, and many believed in the Lord.

After listening to this inspired text, continue seeking its significance and meaning.

Peter must have made frequent pastoral visits to the communities of believers outside Jerusalem. These miracle accounts show Peter on the road to the coastal city of Joppa, on the border of the Jewish homeland and closer to the wider world of the Gentiles. The city of Lydda is about twenty-five miles west of Jerusalem within the Plain of Sharon. Joppa is another day's journey along the coast of the Mediterranean Sea. Peter's apostolic visits are directed to the communities of believers that have already been formed among the Jews of the region. His travels will continue to spread the faith to more and more people.

In Lydda, Peter is introduced to Aeneas, a paralytic who has been confined to his bed for eight years. Peter tells him to arise, making it clear that the risen Jesus is the healer (v. 34). Peter is the mediator of divine healing, an ability he was given during the lifetime of Jesus (Luke 9:1, 6; 10:9). Peter's instruction, "Get up and make your bed," means that Aeneas is restored and can now care for himself. With his new vitality, Aeneas becomes a witness to what Jesus can do so that many residents of the area become believers.

At Joppa, a disciple named Tabitha was known for her good works and charitable giving. She had become sick and died, causing deeply felt grief among the church there. Hearing that Peter is in nearby Lydda, the disciples send emissaries to bring him to Tabitha (v. 38). When Peter arrives at the upstairs room where her body is, the widows are weeping and show him the clothing she had made for them (v. 39).

Peter asks all to leave the room, and he kneels, beseeching God in prayer (v. 40). Peter then turns to the woman and issues the command, "Tabitha, get up." She opens her eyes, sees Peter, and sits up. Peter then offers his hand

and helps her up. When Peter calls the community together and presents her alive, the word spreads, and many more believe in the Lord.

As the writer of both the Gospel of Luke and the Acts of the Apostles, Luke shows clear parallels between the healings of Jesus and those of Peter. The healing of Aeneas is similar to Jesus's cure of the paralytic. Jesus commanded the healed man to get up, pick up his bed, and go home, a similar indication that the man was now able to care for himself (Luke 5:24). Peter's resuscitation of Tabitha echoes similar accounts in the Gospel. At the raising of Jairus's daughter, Jesus cleared the room and commanded the girl to get up (Luke 8:51–55). Peter's words of command in Aramaic would have been, "Tabitha, cumi," which is only slightly different from the traditional words of Jesus to the young girl, "Talitha, cumi." These parallels are no coincidence. Peter's ministry demonstrates that Jesus is still powerfully at work.

While thinking about the commentary on this passage, answer these questions about your reading:

✝ What are the similarities in these two healing accounts?

✝ How do these healing narratives show us the source of Peter's power?

✝ Why does Luke show echoes of Jesus's miracles in these works of Peter?

Meditatio

Consider what Peter is teaching you about the Christian life as you think about the motives and methods of his ministry.

✝ What was the purpose for these healing accounts in the early days of the church? Is healing still an important ministry of the church for the same reasons?

✝ What is the ultimate result of Peter's healing the sick and raising the dead? Why didn't Peter heal everyone he met and raise all those who had died?

✝ In the command to the sick and the dead to "get up," there are echoes of the resurrection of Jesus, the ultimate act of divine power. How do these scenes speak to me about the role of the risen Christ in my life?

Oratio

Offer your prayer to God with the words, ideas, and images from your listening to the Scripture.

> Risen Lord, you restore the sick to health and raise the dead to life. Your power is at work within the ministry of your church as a witness to the saving love of God. Give me a desire to bring your healing peace and loving wholeness to people in the world today.

Continue to pray as your heart directs you . . .

Contemplatio

When thoughts and words are no longer helpful, just fall into the loving hands of God, who desires your wholeness and peace. Simply rest in trusting surrender to God, who heals you from within.

Write a few words about your contemplative experience.

Operatio

Followers of the risen Lord are called to create a culture of life in the world. What can I do to affirm the value of human life and the dignity of every person?

23

The Visions
of Cornelius and Peter

Put away the distractions of the day and enter a quiet place where you can hear God's voice speaking to you through the words of Scripture. Ask the Holy Spirit to fill your heart as you read.

ACTS 10:1–16

[1]In Caesarea there was a man named Cornelius, a centurion of the Italian Cohort, as it was called. [2]He was a devout man who feared God with all his household; he gave alms generously to the people and prayed constantly to God. [3]One afternoon at about three o'clock he had a vision in which he clearly saw an angel of God coming in and saying to him, "Cornelius." [4]He stared at him in terror and said, "What is it, Lord?" He answered, "Your prayers and your alms have ascended as a memorial before God. [5]Now send men to Joppa for a certain Simon who is called Peter; [6]he is lodging with Simon, a tanner, whose house is by the seaside." [7]When the angel who spoke to him had left, he called two of his slaves and a devout soldier from the ranks of those who served him, [8]and after telling them everything, he sent them to Joppa.

⁹About noon the next day, as they were on their journey and approaching the city, Peter went up on the roof to pray. ¹⁰He became hungry and wanted something to eat; and while it was being prepared, he fell into a trance. ¹¹He saw the heaven opened and something like a large sheet coming down, being lowered to the ground by its four corners. ¹²In it were all kinds of four-footed creatures and reptiles and birds of the air. ¹³Then he heard a voice saying, "Get up, Peter; kill and eat." ¹⁴But Peter said, "By no means, Lord; for I have never eaten anything that is profane or unclean." ¹⁵The voice said to him again, a second time, "What God has made clean, you must not call profane." ¹⁶This happened three times, and the thing was suddenly taken up to heaven.

Continue seeking the meaning of this inspired text through the tradition and scholarship of the church.

The events that transpire between Cornelius and Peter mark a major breakthrough in the growing community of disciples and in the development of the Acts of the apostles. The parallel visions of Cornelius and Peter are each received in the context of prayer, emphasizing that the episodes that follow are divinely initiated and directed. God is working in both men: preparing Cornelius to receive the Good News of Jesus Christ and preparing Peter to offer it to him. Through their providential meeting and the conversion of Cornelius, God is leading the church to a broader understanding of itself that will open it to people of all nations.

The disciples of Jesus were continually breaking down the barriers that divided people. Divisions between rich and poor, slave and free, male and female were overcome in the new way of life inspired by Jesus. The first-century church seemed to be a model of freedom and equality. Now the final barrier, the most difficult, was about to be destroyed. The racial, cultural, and religious wall that divided Jews and Gentiles was the supreme test of the power of God's Spirit at work among the early Christians.

Cornelius was truly an outsider. He was a Gentile military officer stationed in Caesarea, the seacoast city that served as the capital of the Roman forces. As such, he represented the oppressive empire that held Israel in subjugation. God was clearly working in the life of an outsider, breaking down the barriers that for so long had been assumed to be God's will.

While the men sent by Cornelius are approaching Joppa, Peter is given a symbolic vision that reveals God's will. In the vision, Peter is shown a smorgasbord of living creatures to satisfy his hunger. Three times Peter is invited to kill and eat the animals presented on the sheet, and Peter protests, saying that he has never eaten anything profane or unclean. The Jewish dietary prohibitions specified in Leviticus 11 distinguish between animals that may be eaten, known as "clean," and animals that may not be eaten, known as "unclean." Yet, in contrast, the heavenly voice insists, "What God has made clean, you must not call profane" (v. 15).

The same prohibitions that separated animals into clean and unclean also divided people from one another. Peter came to realize that his symbolic vision was not only about food laws but also about fellowship and acceptance. It expressed God's will to remove the barriers that divided Jews and Gentiles. If God is making unclean food clean, then Jewish Christians may share table fellowship with Gentiles and cross the barriers that prevented the gospel from being brought to all people.

After studying this text and commentary, respond to these questions to review your understanding:

✝ From the description given of Cornelius, what character traits prepared him to receive the Good News of Jesus Christ?

✝ What is the significance of Peter receiving the vision three times?

Meditatio

Spend some time reflecting on the implications of these visions for your own life and Christian practice.

‡ If Cornelius was an outsider to the believing community, what makes people outsiders to the Christian community today? What perspectives must change in order to invite outsiders to become insiders in Christ?

‡ When we look at other people, we mainly perceive our surface differences. When we look into their core, we recognize our identity. What experiences have taught me this truth?

‡ When has a cultural or religious belief of mine been questioned, challenged, or altered by further evidence or experience?

Oratio

In response to God's speaking to you through Scripture, bring your questions, fears, trust, and confidence to him in prayer.

> Lord God, you have created all creatures, and you rule over all peoples. As you enabled Peter to overcome the barriers that separated him from people longing for the gospel, open my mind to your desire for all people. Help me to be an agent of evangelization and reconciliation in your church.

Continue this prayer in words that issue from your heart ...

Contemplatio

Call to mind the image of a person who is estranged from you or disagreeable to you. Rest with that image, asking God for the gift of wider vision and a transformed heart.

Write a few words about your contemplative experience.

Operatio

What have I learned from Peter about God's working in my own life? What can I do today to break down a barrier between myself and another?

24

Peter Visits
the House of Cornelius

Slowly articulate the words of the inspired text and listen with the ear of your heart. Ask the Holy Spirit to guide your reading.

ACTS 10:17–33

[17]Now while Peter was greatly puzzled about what to make of the vision that he had seen, suddenly the men sent by Cornelius appeared. They were asking for Simon's house and were standing by the gate. [18]They called out to ask whether Simon, who was called Peter, was staying there. [19]While Peter was still thinking about the vision, the Spirit said to him, "Look, three men are searching for you. [20]Now get up, go down, and go with them without hesitation; for I have sent them." [21]So Peter went down to the men and said, "I am the one you are looking for; what is the reason for your coming?" [22]They answered, "Cornelius, a centurion, an upright and God-fearing man, who is well spoken of by the whole Jewish nation, was directed by a holy angel to send for you to come to his house and to hear what you have to say." [23]So Peter invited them in and gave them lodging.

The next day he got up and went with them, and some of the believers from Joppa accompanied him. [24]The following day they came to Caesarea. Cornelius was expecting them and had called together his relatives and close friends. [25]On Peter's arrival Cornelius met him, and falling at his feet, worshiped him. [26]But Peter made him get up, saying, "Stand up; I am only a mortal." [27]And as he talked with him, he went in and found that many had assembled; [28]and he said to them, "You yourselves know that it is unlawful for a Jew to associate with or to visit a Gentile; but God has shown me that I should not call anyone profane or unclean. [29]So when I was sent for, I came without objection. Now may I ask why you sent for me?"

[30]Cornelius replied, "Four days ago at this very hour, at three o'clock, I was praying in my house when suddenly a man in dazzling clothes stood before me. [31]He said, 'Cornelius, your prayer has been heard and your alms have been remembered before God. [32]Send therefore to Joppa and ask for Simon, who is called Peter; he is staying in the home of Simon, a tanner, by the sea.' [33]Therefore I sent for you immediately, and you have been kind enough to come. So now all of us are here in the presence of God to listen to all that the Lord has commanded you to say."

After your reflective reading of the Scripture, continue to search for its meaning and significance in God's plan for the church.

As the narrative unfolds, the action shuttles back and forth between Peter and Cornelius, emphasizing the dual nature of the account. Both men have visions, both exchange stories, both make speeches. The narrative is about the conversion of both Cornelius and Peter; they each must change if the saving plan of God for all people is to go forward.

When the men sent by Cornelius arrive and explain to Peter the purpose of their mission, Peter begins to understand the meaning and purpose of his vision. He hosts the men overnight in preparation for their journey the next day. Meanwhile, Cornelius invites his relatives and friends to his own house to hear what Peter will say. The narrative builds a sense of expectation for Peter's address.

Prompted by God's Spirit, Peter takes the first step in opening the church to Gentiles by walking through the open door of Cornelius's house. Cornelius considers Peter a messenger from God and immediately falls at his feet to worship him. Yet, Peter graciously instructs Cornelius to stand up because he faces a fellow human being (v. 26). Whatever Peter has to offer this Gentile officer, it does not come from himself.

Peter then tells the assembled crowd that entering the home of a Gentile is not customary Jewish practice. Jews had erected firm barriers against Gentiles because of the need to maintain the purity of their belief and worship and to prevent them from being infiltrated by pagan doctrines and practices. Yet, Peter goes on to explain that God has revised his understanding of what is clean and unclean: "God has shown me that I should not call anyone profane or unclean" (v. 28). Peter realizes that his vision was not only about clean and unclean animals but also about people. He knows that the invitation to eat the forbidden animals was also an exhortation to go and stay at the house of Cornelius. Peter now understands that such barriers between Jews and Gentiles no longer serve their original purpose, as God is bringing about a new age of salvation for all.

When Jesus gave Peter the authority to lead his church, Jesus enabled him to guide the practices of the community in ways that would have far-reaching consequences. This pivotal section of Acts shows that Peter is indeed the authoritative guide within the early church as he is moved by the assurance of God's Spirit to open the way of faith to the Gentiles. Though the apostolic mission to all parts of the world would soon be led by Paul, the apostle to the Gentiles, this narrative makes it clear that Peter was the inaugurator of this mission. Paul's missionary activity could take place only after Peter's inspired and decisive action opened the door.

Based on your reading of this meeting of Peter and Cornelius, answer this question:

‡ Why is this meeting between Peter and Cornelius such a critical moment in the development of the Acts of the Apostles?

Meditatio

Bring God's Word into the present context of your life and spend some time reflecting on these questions:

✝ What fuller meaning of his vision of unclean animals did Peter discern when he was led to Cornelius? What might be an extended meaning of Peter's vision for the church today?

✝ In what way does Peter's entering the house of Cornelius demonstrate the importance of his role in the infant church? In what way does Peter pave the way for Paul?

✝ The Spirit of God is about the business of tearing down barriers that divide people. What walls of prejudice and bias prevent the gospel from being truly universal today?

Oratio

Respond to the Word of God you have heard with your own prayer. Pray these words then continue in your own words of prayer:

> Lord of all people, you taught your church to transcend nations, races, genders, and all division. You know the ways in which my mind and heart need conversion. Lead me to see other people as you see them and to offer them the love that you have toward them.

Continue speaking to God as your heart directs . . .

Contemplatio

Place yourself in the presence of the universal God of heaven and earth. As you realize that God's care embraces all people, ask God to give you a share in his love. Be still and feel your heart changing.

Write a few words that arise from your contemplative experience.

Operatio

How are my mind and heart being changed through this biblical narrative? How will my converted mind and heart affect my actions this week?

25

Peter Proclaims
the Gospel to the Gentiles

Lectio

Kiss the words of the biblical text and ask God to let these inspired words
speak powerfully to your spirit today.

ACTS 10:34–48

³⁴Then Peter began to speak to them: "I truly understand that God shows no partiality, ³⁵but in every nation anyone who fears him and does what is right is acceptable to him. ³⁶You know the message he sent to the people of Israel, preaching peace by Jesus Christ—he is Lord of all. ³⁷That message spread throughout Judea, beginning in Galilee after the baptism that John announced: ³⁸how God anointed Jesus of Nazareth with the Holy Spirit and with power; how he went about doing good and healing all who were oppressed by the devil, for God was with him. ³⁹We are witnesses to all that he did both in Judea and in Jerusalem. They put him to death by hanging him on a tree; ⁴⁰but God raised him on the third day and allowed him to appear, ⁴¹not to all the people but to us who were chosen by God as witnesses, and who ate and drank with him after he rose from the dead. ⁴²He commanded us to preach to the people and to testify that he is the one ordained by God as judge of the living and the dead.

⁴³All the prophets testify about him that everyone who believes in him receives forgiveness of sins through his name."

⁴⁴While Peter was still speaking, the Holy Spirit fell upon all who heard the word. ⁴⁵The circumcised believers who had come with Peter were astounded that the gift of the Holy Spirit had been poured out even on the Gentiles, ⁴⁶for they heard them speaking in tongues and extolling God. Then Peter said, ⁴⁷"Can anyone withhold the water for baptizing these people who have received the Holy Spirit just as we have?" ⁴⁸So he ordered them to be baptized in the name of Jesus Christ. Then they invited him to stay for several days.

Continue grappling with the significance of this text through the ongoing tradition of the church.

This sermon in the house of Cornelius is the last example of Peter's preaching offered in Acts. It is his only speech addressed to a Gentile audience. In it Peter shows how the gospel is to be extended beyond the Jewish people to whom it was originally offered to make salvation in Christ available to every believer.

Peter begins with a stunning proclamation: "I truly understand that God shows no partiality" (v. 34). God treats everyone on the same basis, and people from every nation have the same potential access to God. Peter highlights only two characteristics of the person who is acceptable to God: "anyone who fears him and does what is right" (v. 35). Those who treat God with reverence and people with justice are ready for the saving revelation of God through Jesus Christ.

As Peter summarizes the essentials of the Christian message, he emphasizes that Jesus is "Lord of all," Jew and Gentile alike (v. 36). He is expressing the universal will of the risen Christ, that the message of salvation be preached "to all nations, beginning from Jerusalem" (Luke 24:47). This great commission of Jesus given to his disciples is beginning to be realized as the saving news extends beyond Jerusalem and is destined for all the nations of the world.

The proclamation of the Good News can be just meaningless words for a person who is not ready to receive it. It is only the message of salvation for a person who is searching and realizes the need for God. Cornelius had been seeking God for a long time. He had already begun to pray and to do good for those in need. God had been preparing his mind and heart for the message he is now receiving from Peter. Through the preached gospel, Cornelius went from open seeker to confirmed believer.

As Peter is still speaking, proclaiming forgiveness of sins to everyone who believes, the Holy Spirit is given to Cornelius and the other Gentiles who are listening to Peter (v. 44). The Jews who had come with Peter are amazed that "the gift of the Holy Spirit had been poured out even on the Gentiles" (v. 45). The coming of God's promised Spirit is the sign of the new era, and this event has rightly been called the Pentecost of the Gentile world.

Peter understands the significance of the moment, and he instructs that the Gentiles be baptized in the name of Jesus Christ (v. 48). Jews and Gentiles are equal in Christ; their need and God's answer to that need are the same. Peter receives hospitality and shares table fellowship for several days with these uncircumcised Christians. Peter is the primary instrument of God's epoch-making work, showing that the Gentiles too are chosen for salvation, baptism, and membership in Christ's church. The gospel is now ready to go out into the entire world.

After reading Peter's sermon in the household of Cornelius, consider these questions:

✝ What did Peter mean when he stated that God shows no partiality?

✝ Why is it significant that Peter is God's instrument in bringing salvation in Christ to the first Gentiles?

Meditatio

Consider what you are learning from this scene in your continuing efforts to be a faithful disciple like Peter.

‡ Why is the Good News of Jesus just meaningless words for some people? What is necessary for those saving words to lead to conversion?

‡ The church is catholic and apostolic because it encompasses the whole world and is rooted in the tradition of the apostles. What direction is needed in the Christian community today so that it can more fully become one, holy, catholic, and apostolic church?

‡ What might Peter have done in the household of Cornelius during the several days he stayed with him? What is necessary for new Christians after the initial experience of salvation and baptism?

Oratio

Offer your prayer to God in response to this dramatic scene in the house of Cornelius. Express the desires, hopes, and gratitude that fill your own heart.

> Savior of all nations, I can sometimes become very comfortable in my own culture, my own neighborhood, and my own biases. Yet you call your disciples to remove barriers and open doors that separate people from one another. Give me a vision of your all-inclusive kingdom.

Continue to pray in your own words . . .

Contemplatio

Consider that God sees all people with unconditional positive regard and unimaginable love. Spend a few moments in wordless prayer, seeking to receive a share of God's own universal love.

After your time of quiet, choose a few words that express the fruits of your silent contemplation.

Operatio

As a disciple of Jesus, I am called to participate in the outward mission of the church to the world. What can I do to support the missionary activity of the church?

26

Peter Is Set Free
from Prison

Lectio

Read this account aloud so that you can better imagine the scene and enter its drama.

ACTS 12:1–19

¹About that time King Herod laid violent hands upon some who belonged to the church. ²He had James, the brother of John, killed with the sword. ³After he saw that it pleased the Jews, he proceeded to arrest Peter also. (This was during the festival of Unleavened Bread.) ⁴When he had seized him, he put him in prison and handed him over to four squads of soldiers to guard him, intending to bring him out to the people after the Passover. ⁵While Peter was kept in prison, the church prayed fervently to God for him. ⁶The very night before Herod was going to bring him out, Peter, bound with two chains, was sleeping between two soldiers, while guards in front of the door were keeping watch over the prison. ⁷Suddenly an angel of the Lord appeared and a light shone in the cell. He tapped Peter on the side and woke him, saying, "Get up quickly." And the chains fell off his wrists. ⁸The angel said to him, "Fasten your belt and put on your sandals." He did so. Then he said to him, "Wrap your cloak around

you and follow me." [9]Peter went out and followed him; he did not realize that what was happening with the angel's help was real; he thought he was seeing a vision. [10]After they had passed the first and the second guard, they came before the iron gate leading into the city. It opened for them of its own accord, and they went outside and walked along a lane, when suddenly the angel left him. [11]Then Peter came to himself and said, "Now I am sure that the Lord has sent his angel and rescued me from the hands of Herod and from all that the Jewish people were expecting."

[12]As soon as he realized this, he went to the house of Mary, the mother of John whose other name was Mark, where many had gathered and were praying. [13]When he knocked at the outer gate, a maid named Rhoda came to answer. [14]On recognizing Peter's voice, she was so overjoyed that, instead of opening the gate, she ran in and announced that Peter was standing at the gate. [15]They said to her, "You are out of your mind!" But she insisted that it was so. They said, "It is his angel." [16]Meanwhile Peter continued knocking; and when they opened the gate, they saw him and were amazed. [17]He motioned to them with his hand to be silent, and described for them how the Lord had brought him out of the prison. And he added, "Tell this to James and to the believers." Then he left and went to another place.

[18]When morning came, there was no small commotion among the soldiers over what had become of Peter. [19]When Herod had searched for him and could not find him, he examined the guards and ordered them to be put to death. Then Peter went down from Judea to Caesarea and stayed there.

Having listened to this dramatic rescue, continue your search for its meaning for the church.

The persecution of the church in Jerusalem grew in intensity, first from the religious authorities and then from the civil government of Herod Agrippa. The ruler desired to annihilate the Christian movement by striking at its highest leadership. He had James the apostle beheaded with a sword, and he targeted Peter with the same fate. Peter was arrested and imprisoned during the same Jewish feast on which Jesus was put to death. Herod planned to bring Peter before the people after Passover to face judgment and be executed.

Peter is held in maximum security, with one soldier chained to each of his arms and two others guarding the door. Meanwhile, the church is praying fervently for him (v. 5). At the last moment, the night before Peter is to appear for judgment, God acts through the ministry of an angel to rescue him (vv. 6–7). With a shining light, God rescues him from the darkness and liberates him from imminent death. Peter emerges from the prison alive, and he goes off to tell the disciples the good news.

After being freed, Peter goes to the house where the disciples are meeting and knocks on the door. With comic detail, the writer describes how the servant girl, Rhoda, is so excited at realizing it is Peter that she forgets to open the door (vv. 13–14). Instead, she rushes off to tell the community of believers who are gathered inside. While they argue for a while over Rhoda's sanity, Peter continues to knock at the door. When he is finally allowed in the house, Peter tells the astonished crowd what happened.

The next morning the guards are totally confused (v. 18). Each blaming the other, they are flabbergasted by the empty chains beside them. Quite a commotion is raised as Herod searches for Peter and cannot find his prized prisoner. The writer contrasts the scene of the believers in the house of John Mark with that of the baffled guards in the prison. The one is a scene of bewildered joy and gratitude; the other is a scene of revenge and punishment. While the Christians praise God for Peter's deliverance, the Roman guards are put to death.

This episode of persecution explains why Peter left his leadership position in the church in Jerusalem and goes "to another place" (v. 17). His parting words are a request to explain to James, the brother of Jesus, and the rest of the believers what happened. This James will become the leading figure in the Jerusalem church, while Peter becomes a traveling missionary in other parts of the world.

Answer this question based on your reading:

‡ Why would the Christian community enjoy telling this story for many years?

Meditatio

Allow the scene to interact with your own world of ideas, concerns, thoughts, and feelings. Consider the deeper significance of this text for your life within the church.

✝ Throughout the Bible, God delivers his people from bondage. What parallels to Peter's rescue have I seen in the way God has acted in my life?

✝ Surely the church in Jerusalem prayed for the release of James the apostle just as it prayed for Peter's release. Why did God allow James to be martyred while he delivered Peter from imprisonment and death? Why does the church often experience new life in the midst of persecution?

✝ The Acts of the Apostles continually shows us how the life, death, and resurrection of Jesus are reflected and renewed within the church. In what ways does this account demonstrate that the power of Christ's saving death and resurrection is at work in the ministry of Peter?

Oratio

Respond in prayerful gratitude to the saving work of God within the lives of his people.

> Liberating God, you rescue your people from the bondage of slavery, sickness, sin, hopelessness, and death. I thank you for the ways you have freed me from oppressive power that I am unable to control. Help me to live with gratitude in the new life you have given me.

Continue offering prayers to God in whatever ways seem to respond to the divine Word spoken to you . . .

Contemplatio

In wordless silence, give to God those aspects of your life over which you have no control. Trust that God will hear your prayers and respond to your need in a way that is ultimately good for you.

Write a few words about your contemplative experience.

Operatio

Peter was freed from prison because he responded to God's lead. In what aspect of my life should I admit my own powerlessness and surrender to the Highest Power to show me the way?

27

The Apostolic Council
at Jerusalem

Ask the Holy Spirit to guide your listening to this text as the Spirit led the apostles in Jerusalem. Invoke that same Spirit of God to anoint your mind, lips, and heart as you read this inspired Scripture.

ACTS 15:1–12

¹Then certain individuals came down from Judea and were teaching the brothers, "Unless you are circumcised according to the custom of Moses, you cannot be saved." ²And after Paul and Barnabas had no small dissension and debate with them, Paul and Barnabas and some of the others were appointed to go up to Jerusalem to discuss this question with the apostles and the elders. ³So they were sent on their way by the church, and as they passed through both Phoenicia and Samaria, they reported the conversion of the Gentiles, and brought great joy to all the believers. ⁴When they came to Jerusalem, they were welcomed by the church and the apostles and the elders, and they reported all that God had done with them. ⁵But some believers who belonged to the sect of the Pharisees stood up and said, "It is necessary for them to be circumcised and ordered to keep the law of Moses."

⁶The apostles and the elders met together to consider this matter. ⁷After there had been much debate, Peter stood up and said to them, "My brothers, you know that in the early days God made a choice among you, that I should be the one through whom the Gentiles would hear the message of the good news and become believers. ⁸And God, who knows the human heart, testified to them by giving them the Holy Spirit, just as he did to us; ⁹and in cleansing their hearts by faith he has made no distinction between them and us. ¹⁰Now therefore why are you putting God to the test by placing on the neck of the disciples a yoke that neither our ancestors nor we have been able to bear? ¹¹On the contrary, we believe that we will be saved through the grace of the Lord Jesus, just as they will."

¹²The whole assembly kept silence, and listened to Barnabas and Paul as they told of all the signs and wonders that God had done through them among the Gentiles.

Continue exploring the significance of this council of the apostles for the expanding church.

This gathering of church leaders in Jerusalem is often called a council, the prototype of later church councils called to settle a particularly troublesome controversy and to unify the church in its mission. The issue in question here involves the inclusion of Gentiles in the new community. The debate is not whether Gentiles should be received into the church but on what basis they should be included. The key question to be resolved is whether Gentiles must become Jewish to be genuinely Christian.

The controversy has incited "no small dissension and debate" and is causing deep divisions within the church (v. 2). Some of the Jewish Christians insist that circumcision and practicing the ordinances of the Torah are foundational to covenant faithfulness and a necessary part of being God's people. Paul and Barnabas hold the opposite view, that Gentiles should not be required to practice the ritual precepts of the Torah. The conversion of Gentiles is the work of God's grace through Jesus Christ, irrespective of practicing the law of Moses.

It is clear from the structure of the council that the solution will not come from Paul and Barnabas or from those opposing them but from the apostles and elders in Jerusalem. The issue is too important to be left to local debate, and it must be a decision for the whole church. A definitive, churchwide resolution of this issue is essential for the church's ongoing mission.

After considerable debate among the apostles and elders, Peter stands to speak (v. 7). He places the emphasis on God's initiative, as he reviews his experience with the household of Cornelius. Peter was the first to preach the gospel and call Gentiles to faith. He stresses that God's gift of the Spirit was given to them just as it had been given to Jewish believers at Pentecost (v. 8). In terms of access to salvation, there is no distinction between Jews and Gentiles. Peter's conclusion states the principle at the heart of the council's pronouncement: both Jews and Gentiles "will be saved through the grace of the Lord Jesus" (v. 11). Since it is God who purifies the hearts of both Jews and Gentiles through faith, the church should put no unnecessary obstacles in the way to salvation.

This scene marks Peter's last appearance in the Acts of the Apostles. The council completely legitimates the Gentile mission and the full inclusion of Gentiles in the church. It does not resolve every issue, but it forms a firm basis for the work narrated in the second half of Acts. From here on, the primary action of the book is the gospel going out to the ends of the earth through the work of Paul. Through the mission of Peter and Paul, the church becomes the instrument of salvation in bringing people of every nation to Christ.

After reading this account of the Jerusalem council, seek to answer these questions:

✝ What are the primary issues at stake in the early church as reflected in this narrative?

✝ Why is it significant to the council that Peter, rather than Paul, initiated the conversion of the Gentiles?

Meditatio

Reflect on the implications of this central passage of Acts for the church today and for your discipleship.

‡ How is the leadership of Peter among the apostles manifested at this council in Jerusalem? Why is authoritative and collaborative leadership an important element in the nature of the church?

‡ Why was this controversy so difficult for Peter to mediate, given the fact that Peter is a faithful Jew? What has Peter learned since his experience with Cornelius?

‡ Why is Peter's insight about God's inclusive grace so critical for the mission of the church? What are its implications for my discipleship?

Oratio

Ask that the Holy Spirit, who guided your listening to God's Word, will lead your response to that Word in prayer.

Creator God, we believe that you offer salvation to all the peoples of the earth through the grace of the Lord Jesus. Pour your Holy Spirit into my heart and give me a passion for the gospel and for the mission of your church.

Continue to pray to God through the working of the Holy Spirit within you.

Contemplatio

Rest with security in God's saving grace at work within your heart. Spend a few moments seeking to experience the confident assurance of a child of God.

Write a few words that linger from your silent time in God's presence.

Operatio

Why is it important to understand Scripture in light of my ongoing life experiences? What practical ideas can I learn from Peter in this regard?

28

Peter Encounters Paul in Jerusalem and Antioch

Lectio

Listen to these words of Paul as he describes his relationship with Peter. Consider the thoughts and emotions that the letter records.

GALATIANS 2:7–16

⁷When they saw that I [Paul] had been entrusted with the gospel for the uncircumcised, just as Peter had been entrusted with the gospel for the circumcised ⁸(for he who worked through Peter making him an apostle to the circumcised also worked through me in sending me to the Gentiles), ⁹and when James and Cephas and John, who were acknowledged pillars, recognized the grace that had been given to me, they gave to Barnabas and me the right hand of fellowship, agreeing that we should go to the Gentiles and they to the circumcised. ¹⁰They asked only one thing, that we remember the poor, which was actually what I was eager to do.

¹¹But when Cephas came to Antioch, I opposed him to his face, because he stood self-condemned; ¹²for until certain people came from James, he used to eat with the Gentiles. But after they came, he drew back and kept himself separate for fear of the circumcision faction. · ¹³And the other Jews joined him in this hypocrisy, so that even Barna-

bas was led astray by their hypocrisy. ¹⁴But when I saw that they were not acting consistently with the truth of the gospel, I said to Cephas before them all, "If you, though a Jew, live like a Gentile and not like a Jew, how can you compel the Gentiles to live like Jews?"

¹⁵We ourselves are Jews by birth and not Gentile sinners; ¹⁶yet we know that a person is justified not by the works of the law but through faith in Jesus Christ. And we have come to believe in Christ Jesus, so that we might be justified by faith in Christ, and not by doing the works of the law, because no one will be justified by the works of the law.

After listening to the words of Paul's letter, continue exploring their significance for our understanding of the early church.

This letter of Paul, written to his Gentile converts in Galatia, reveals much about Paul's relationship to Peter. Paul writes in defense of the gospel he had proclaimed in the face of Jewish Christians seeking to undermine his authority. These agitators had asserted the necessity of becoming a Jew before becoming a Christian. They had insisted on the believers' obligation to accept circumcision, practice Jewish food laws, and follow the other duties of the Torah. In response to this challenge, Paul writes about two of his meetings with Peter, one in Jerusalem and another in Antioch, in order to convince the believers of his apostolic authority and to help persuade them to accept his understanding of the gospel.

Paul first describes the agreement he reached with the leaders of the Jerusalem church. These leading apostles acknowledged that Paul had been entrusted by God with preaching the gospel to the uncircumcised Gentiles just as Peter had been assigned the evangelization of the circumcised Jews (vv. 7–9). This division of labor was not clear-cut because Peter had certainly ministered among Gentiles and Paul preached to both Jews and Gentiles during his travels. However, as a generally accepted division of responsibilities for the gospel, Peter and Paul served in these complementary apostolic roles. Since James, Peter, and John—the apostolic "pillars" of the mother church in Jerusalem—had approved Paul's understanding of the gospel, they had affirmed that there is no necessity for Gentile converts to be circumcised.

Paul then describes his encounter with Cephas in Antioch, a community made up of both Jewish and Gentile believers. "Cephas" is Aramaic for "rock" and the way that Paul most often identifies Peter. Paul states that Peter formerly ate with Gentiles as a regular practice when shepherding the church there. However, when Jewish Christians came from James in Jerusalem to visit, they persuaded Peter, along with Barnabas and other Jewish Christians, to withdraw from table fellowship with the Gentiles. In response, Paul opposed Peter and accused him of hypocrisy (vv. 11–14). Because Peter had agreed with Paul in principle that the Gentiles were freed from following the precepts of the Torah, Paul declared Peter's actions inconsistent with his beliefs and accused him of compromising the freedom that the Gentiles had been given in Christ.

Because Paul's letter gives us only Paul's point of view, we are not given the perspective of Peter. Clearly the agreement in Jerusalem had not settled all the issues regarding the relationship between Jewish and Gentile converts in a mixed community. As apostle to the Jews, Peter knows that many Jewish believers continue to demonstrate loyalty to the covenant laws and ancestral customs that constituted their Jewish identity. Out of concern for his own mission to the circumcised, he chose to honor the deeply felt beliefs of his fellow Jews. The truth of the gospel, Peter felt, was not at stake. Paul, however, strongly disagreed.

While he clearly respects the authority of Peter, Paul's passionate nature and strong belief in principles convince him to challenge Peter for not "acting consistently with the truth of the gospel" (v. 14). The heart of the matter, as Paul sees it, is that Christians are made right before God not through what they themselves accomplish but through what Jesus Christ has done. As Paul writes in his timeless statement, "a person is justified not by the works of the law but through faith in Jesus Christ" (v. 16). By rebuking Peter publicly, he stands strong for this basic principle of all followers of Jesus—both Jew and Gentile. The confrontation between Peter and Paul demonstrates the challenges of pastoral leadership and its need for continual adjustment and sometimes correction.

Meditatio

Consider the tensions and disagreement between Paul and Peter as demonstrated in this letter in light of the struggles of the church today.

‡ What issues of tension in the church today might be similar to the early struggles involved in joining Jews and Gentiles into one church? Are there any principles that we can learn from Peter and Paul?

‡ People seeking unity within diversity for the church often refer to an ancient pastoral adage: "In essentials unity, in doubtful things liberty, but in all things charity." In what way does the struggle in Antioch illustrate this ancient wisdom?

‡ Peter is frequently seen as a middle way between the party of James in Jerusalem and the followers of Paul in the tug-of-war between principle and pragmatism. Why are dialogue and compromise so important in the pastoral life of the church today?

Oratio

Having listened to God speaking through this account of the early church, respond in prayer, using some of the same vocabulary and emotions that fill this Scripture.

> Merciful Lord, you appointed Peter and Paul as the great apostles to the Jews and Gentiles. Give me the compassion of a shepherd and the zeal of a preacher to spread your gospel to the world. Teach me how to compromise and how to stand firm.

Continue praying in whatever words seem to express the content of your heart . . .

Contemplatio

Peter and Paul inspire us with their dedication, compassion, sensitivity, courage, fervor, and zeal. In your time of silence, ask God to fill you with whatever you need for the service of the gospel. Let God work deep within your heart.

Write a few words about your experience of God's interior work.

Operatio

Like Peter and Paul, all disciples are sent out into the world to cultivate a spirit of mission for the gospel. How can I develop the heart of a missionary within the context of my own life?

29

The Church
Is a Living Temple

Listen to the words of Peter's letter about Christ and his church. Slowly artic-ulate the words and recall all the generations of Christians who have heard these words before you.

1 PETER 2:4–10

⁴Come to him, a living stone, though rejected by mortals yet chosen and precious in God's sight, and ⁵like living stones, let yourselves be built into a spiritual house, to be a holy priesthood, to offer spiritual sacrifices acceptable to God through Jesus Christ. ⁶For it stands in scripture:

"See, I am laying in Zion a stone,
a cornerstone chosen and precious;
and whoever believes in him will not be put to shame."

⁷To you then who believe, he is precious; but for those who do not believe,

"The stone that the builders rejected
has become the very head of the corner,"
⁸and

"A stone that makes them stumble,
and a rock that makes them fall."
They stumble because they disobey the word, as they were destined to do.

⁹But you are a chosen race, a royal priesthood, a holy nation, God's own people, in order that you may proclaim the mighty acts of him who called you out of darkness into his marvelous light.

¹⁰Once you were not a people,
but now you are God's people;
once you had not received mercy,
but now you have received mercy.

Continue exploring this letter in search of its implications for all God's people.

This letter is pastoral in tone, written to be circulated among the churches of Asia Minor (today's Turkey) and designed to build up the faith of its readers. If it was written by Peter himself, he wrote it with the help of his secretary Silvanus (5:12) in the city of Rome shortly before Peter's martyrdom there. If it was written after his death, it is a short compendium of Peter's teachings written in his name by one of his disciples. In either case, it represents a magnificent statement of Peter's apostolic zeal for the churches to help them face the challenges of living in a hostile world.

Peter's legacy indicates that he took his missionary mandate to his fellow Jews seriously. His influence on Jewish believers was tremendously important in keeping Christianity within the framework of ancient Israel and ensuring that its Jewish character was not lost. The letter is soaked with quotations, allusions, and images from the Hebrew Scriptures. Furthermore, it shows evidence that Peter reflected on the teachings, suffering, death, and resurrection of Jesus and considered their meaning and significance for the infant church.

Peter, the Rock, uses a similar image, the "stone," to reflect on Christ and his relationship to the church. He offers three Old Testament texts to illustrate his variations on the stone theme. The first is Psalm 118:22, used by Jesus in the gospels to refer to himself: "The stone that the builders rejected has become the cornerstone" (Matt. 21:42). The second is Isaiah 28:16 which amplifies the image of Jesus as the most important stone of the construction: "See, I am laying in Zion a foundation stone, a tested stone, a precious cornerstone, a sure foundation." A third text, Isaiah 8:14, describes Jesus in relationship to those who reject him: he becomes "a stone that makes them stumble, and a rock that makes them fall" (v. 8).

According to God's grand design for the church, we are "like living stones" being built upon the foundation stone of Jesus into a spiritual house (v. 5). As individual believers are built up in faith, each one becomes an integral part of God's house, according to the divine architectural plan. This holy temple exists for the singular purpose of worshiping God. In contrast to the temple of ancient Israel, made of lifeless stones, this spiritual house is made of living stones. Rather than an inherited priesthood made up only of Levites, all Christians form a holy priesthood. Instead of material sacrifices, Christians offer spiritual sacrifices of prayer and praise, of self-consecration and self-giving. Such sacrifices are acceptable to God not on account of the one offering them but because they are made "through Jesus Christ," that is, joined with his perfect sacrifice and united with his Spirit.

To this wonderful image of the church, Peter adds more: "You are a chosen race, a royal priesthood, a holy nation, God's own people" (v. 9). These images are all derived from Exodus 19:5–6. As God's chosen ones, the church is the heir to the promises God made to his people of old. In applying these sacred titles to the church, Peter recognizes that God's grand narrative of salvation is continued and fulfilled through the community of Christian believers.

Summarize your understanding of Peter's letter by answering these questions:

✝ What in this letter indicates that Peter focused his missionary efforts on the Jewish people?

✝ How does a Christian offer "spiritual sacrifices acceptable to God" (v. 5)?

Reflect on the images and ideas contained in this letter of Peter. Allow these words to give you confidence in the divine institution of Christ's church.

✝ As Jesus tells Peter that he is the Rock, Peter tells us who we are. What words of Peter are most important to me in understanding my identity as a Christian?

✝ Why does Peter include so many quotations from the Psalms and Prophets in his letter? Why is it critically important for me to know the Old Testament in order to understand the New?

✝ Peter writes his letter to communities of faith living in a hostile world. What do I find most comforting and encouraging in this passage for my life today?

Oratio

Pray in response to God's Word delivered through the first letter of Peter.

Lord God of Israel, you call your church to be a spiritual house made of living stones, a royal priesthood, and your own people. Teach me to proclaim your mighty deeds and to offer spiritual sacrifices through your Son Jesus.

Continue to pray as the Holy Spirit prompts you . . .

Contemplatio

Choose one of the images by which Peter has identified you. Slowly repeat that title as you contemplate God's formative power working within you.

Write a few words to conclude your time of contemplation.

Operatio

As part of God's royal priesthood, what spiritual sacrifice can I offer God today?

30

Shepherding the Flock of God

Lectio

Listen to Peter's final exhortation from Rome. Consider the expectation it offers for all people and the hope it embodies for you.

1 PETER 5:1–11

¹Now as an elder myself and a witness of the sufferings of Christ, as well as one who shares in the glory to be revealed, I exhort the elders among you ²to tend the flock of God that is in your charge, exercising the oversight, not under compulsion but willingly, as God would have you do it—not for sordid gain but eagerly. ³Do not lord it over those in your charge, but be examples to the flock. ⁴And when the chief shepherd appears, you will win the crown of glory that never fades away. ⁵In the same way, you who are younger must accept the authority of the elders. And all of you must clothe yourselves with humility in your dealings with one another, for

"God opposes the proud,
but gives grace to the humble."

⁶Humble yourselves therefore under the mighty hand of God, so that he may exalt you in due time. ⁷Cast all your anxiety on him, because he cares for you. ⁸Discipline yourselves, keep alert. Like a roaring

lion your adversary the devil prowls around, looking for someone to devour. ⁹Resist him, steadfast in your faith, for you know that your brothers and sisters in all the world are undergoing the same kinds of suffering. ¹⁰And after you have suffered for a little while, the God of all grace, who has called you to his eternal glory in Christ, will himself restore, support, strengthen, and establish you. ¹¹To him be the power forever and ever. Amen.

After listening to Peter's letter, consider the ongoing meaning of these inspired words.

Peter calls Jesus the "chief shepherd" (v. 4) and understands his own leadership within the church as modeled on the life of Jesus. By the time Peter wrote this letter, Jesus's charge to him, "Tend my sheep" (John 21:16), had been fulfilled for several decades through Peter's pastoral care of the church in many areas of the world. Peter's charge to the pastors of the church, "Tend the flock of God that is in your charge" (v. 2), reflects his own experience of suffering and joy among the "flock of God."

In offering his pastoral advice, Peter reminds the elders that they do not own the flock; rather, they exercise "oversight" of God's flock. He describes the kind of leadership they should exercise through a series of contrasts. They should shepherd the community not under compulsion but willingly, not inspired by greed but by a desire for service, and not lording it over them but by being "examples to the flock" (vv. 2–3). The image of Christ the Shepherd must encourage them to act like shepherds to all entrusted to their care.

The final section of the letter is directed to all of Peter's listeners and consists of a series of imperatives: humble yourselves, cast all your anxiety on God, discipline yourselves, keep alert, and resist your adversary, the devil (vv. 6–9). Despite the suffering of the present age, God still remains in control of events. Because the devil is constantly prowling like a ferocious lion, we must oppose him, but not with our own power. We must stand firm in our faith, because our adversary is conquered only with the power of Christ. God is using every experience, especially that of suffering, to further his loving purpose in our lives and to enable us to grow in grace.

Because we know that God cares personally about his people, we can rely on God's power to deliver his own when the time is right.

Peter's letter shows the strong bonds that joined the early communities of the church stretched out across the world. From the church in Rome, Peter reaches out to the small towns in the remote provinces of Asia Minor. He reminds them that they are not alone but that they are part of a worldwide church united together in suffering and in hope. The struggles of believers are necessary to following Christ, but they are part of the transformation through which evil will be overcome and through which believers will share in God's eternal glory in Christ (v. 10).

Early Christian evidence testifies that Peter met his death in Rome. Jesus had said that a good shepherd is willing even to die for his sheep. Peter's care for the flock met its greatest test during the persecutions begun by the emperor Nero. Writing from the heart of the Roman Empire, Peter proclaimed to the distant churches that he was "a witness of the sufferings of Christ" (v. 1). For Peter his final and greatest act of witness was his death as a martyr for Christ.

After reading this inspired text, synthesize your experience of lectio by answering these questions:

‡ In what way does Peter suggest that Christ's church is not just local but universal?

‡ What does Peter urge Christians to do during periods of trial and suffering?

Meditatio

Think about the implications of Peter's letter to the churches for your own faith in the present and hope in the future.

‡ What, according to Peter, are some bad reasons for being in church leadership? What are the good motives that Peter urges leaders to cultivate? Which of these motives have I seen in pastoral ministry?

‡ Why is the image of the shepherd used by the prophets, Jesus, and Peter when describing the earthly care of God's people? What are the qualities and best practices of a good shepherd?

‡ What forms of spiritual discipline do I need to practice in order to resist the devil, who prowls around, looking for someone to devour? What advice of Peter must I remember in this regard?

Oratio

Respond in prayer to God's Word spoken to you through Peter's inspired letter.

> God of all grace, you challenge us to keep alert, to discipline ourselves, to be humble, and to cast our anxieties on you. We know that our suffering is only for a little while, and we trust that you have called us to your eternal glory in Christ. To him be the power forever and ever.

When words are no longer helpful or necessary, move into the wordless prayer of contemplatio.

Contemplatio

Peter tells us to cast all our anxiety on God. In wordless quiet, give your fears and worries over to God. In silent trust, realize that God cares for you. Rest in the knowledge that God holds your life in his hands.

What words come to mind after your contemplative time in God's presence?

Operatio

How has this study of Peter shaped and changed me? What do I most want to remember and incorporate into my life?

Ancient-Future Bible
Study for Small Groups

A small group for *collatio*, the communal practice of lectio divina, is a wonderful way to let the power of Scripture more deeply nourish participants. Through the thoughts, reflections, prayers, and experiences of the other members of the group, each individual comes to understand Scripture more intensely and experience it more profoundly. By sharing our understanding and wisdom in a faith-filled group of people, we discover how to let God live in every dimension of our lives and we enrich the lives of others.

These groups may be formed in any number of ways, just as you create groups for other learning experiences within your community. Groups composed of no more than a dozen people are best for this experience. It is preferable to give people with various needs a variety of days and times from which to choose.

Small groups are best formed when people are encouraged and supported by a church's pastoral leadership and personally welcomed into these small communities. Personally directed invitations are most effective for convincing people to add another dimension to their schedules.

The collatio should never take the place of one's regular, personal lectio divina. Rather, a weekly communal practice is an ideal extension and continuation of personal, daily sacred reading. At each group session, participants discuss the fruits of their individual lectio divina and practice elements of lectio divina together.

Participants should read carefully the opening sections of this book before joining the group. "The Movements of Lectio Divina," "The Essence of

Lectio Divina," and "Your Personal Practice of Ancient-Future Bible Study" would be helpful sections to review throughout the course of the study.

The full weekly collatio group session is designed for about ninety minutes. Those groups with limited time may choose either Part 1 or Part 2 for the group experience. Instructions for each of the collatio groups are provided on the following pages.

Suggestions for Participating in the Group

‡ The spirit of the collatio should be that of a personal conversation, with the members desiring to learn from one another and building each other up. The divine Word is the teacher; the members of the group are all learners.

‡ When participating in the group, members should offer their thoughts, insights, and feelings about the sacred text. The group can avoid the distraction of off-topic chatter by sticking to the text, the commentary, and their personal response to the text from the meditatio.

‡ Group members should be careful to give everyone in the group an opportunity to share. When discussing personal thoughts, members should use "I" language and be cautious about giving advice to others. They should listen attentively to the other members of the group so as to learn from their insights and should not worry about trying to cover all the questions in each gathering. They should select only those that seem the most helpful for group discussion.

‡ Dispute, debate, and dogmatic hairsplitting within the group erode its focus and purpose. Opposition and division destroy the supportive bond of the group. The desire of individuals to assert themselves and their own ideas wears down the spirit of the group. In a community setting, it is often wise to "agree to disagree." An inflexible, pedantic attitude blocks the way to a vital and fulfilling understanding of the passage. The Scriptures are the living Word of God, the full meaning of which we can never exhaust.

‡ It is usually helpful to have someone to guide the process of the group. This facilitator directs the discussion, helping the group keep the discussion on time and on track. The facilitator need not be an expert, either in Scripture or in the process of lectio divina, but simply a person with the skills necessary to guide a group. This role may be rotated among members of the group, if desired.

Group Study in Six Sessions

- Begin each group session with hospitality and welcome. Name tags are helpful if group members don't know one another. Offer any announcements or instructions before entering the spirit of prayer.

- Set the tone and focus the group by saying the gathering prayer together.

- Note that the first group session is a bit different from the others because it involves reading and discussing the introduction. After the first group session, all the remaining sessions follow the same format.

- The group sessions are in two parts. Part 1 is a discussion of the fruits of the lectio divina that participants completed on their own since the last group session. To provoke personal discussion of each chapter, ask this question: "What insight is most significant to you from your reflection on this chapter?" Group members may mention insights they gained in the lectio, meditatio, oratio, contemplatio, or operatio of each chapter.

- Part 2 is a session of lectio divina in the group. Leave at least half of the group time for this section. Move through each of the five movements as described in the chapter. Read the text aloud, followed by the commentary. Leave the most time for the more personal questions of the meditatio. Don't worry if you don't complete them all.

- Leave sufficient time for the oratio, contemplatio, and operatio. These movements should not be rushed. Gently guide the group from vocal prayer into a period of restful silence. Don't neglect to conclude the lectio divina by mentioning some practical fruits of operatio before dismissing the group into the world of daily discipleship.

- Conclude each group session by encouraging participants to complete the lectio divina on their own for the upcoming chapters. Ask them to write their responses to each movement of lectio in their book.

Collatio Group 1

‡ The first group session is a bit different from the others. After offering greetings and introductions, explain the process of Ancient-Future Bible Study. Then set the tone for the group experience by praying together the gathering prayer.

‡ Gathering prayer:

> *Come upon us, Holy Spirit, to enlighten and guide us as we begin this study of* Peter: Fisherman and Shepherd of the Church. *You have inspired the biblical authors to give to your people a living Word that has the power to convert our hearts and change our lives. Give us a sense of expectation, trusting that you will shine the light of your truth within us. Bless us as we gather with your gifts of wisdom and discernment so that we may listen to the inspired Word and experience its transforming energy.*

‡ Spend the first half of the collatio group reading the introduction to this book and discussing the questions to consider. A volunteer may read each section aloud, and the group will spend a few minutes discussing the questions that follow.

‡ Spend the second half of the group time following the five movements of the lectio divina at the end of the introduction. Read the text aloud, followed by the commentary. Then spend time reflecting and sharing responses to the questions of the meditatio.

‡ When leading into the oratio, pray the prayer aloud, then leave time for additional prayers from the group. When the vocal prayer has receded, lead the group into contemplatio. Help the group to feel comfortable with the quiet and relax in the presence of God. Conclude the lectio divina with the operatio. Share encouragement and commitment to practice lectio divina throughout the week.

‡ Before departing, instruct group members in their practice of lectio divina during the week. Participants should complete the lectio divina for chapters 1–5 for next week. Encourage them to write their responses to each movement of lectio in their book. The lectio divina for chapter 6 will be done together in the group next week.

Collatio Group 2

✝ Gathering prayer:

> *Creating and redeeming God, when your Son Jesus began to proclaim your kingdom, he called Peter to be his first disciple, to be a fisher of men and women, and to be the solid foundation of his church. Help us to realize that Jesus also calls us to follow him, to evangelize in word and deed, and to extend his work in the world today. When our challenges seem impossible, may we look to Peter as a mentor and guide as we call upon Jesus as Messiah and Lord.*

✝ Part 1:
- Having completed the lectio divina for chapters 1–5 during the week, the group members discuss the fruit of their practice for these five chapters. Divide the chapters into equal time allotments so that no chapter is neglected. To provoke personal discussion of each chapter, ask this question: "What insight is most significant to you from your reflection on this chapter?"

✝ Part 2:
- Spend at least the last half of the group time in the full lectio divina of chapter 6. Move through each step according to the instructions provided in the chapter, leaving plenty of time for oratio, contemplatio, and operatio.

✝ Departure:
- Encourage participants to complete the lectio divina for chapters 7–11 before the next collatio group. Ask them to write their responses to each movement of lectio in their book. The lectio divina for chapter 12 will be done together in the group next week.

Collatio Group 3

✝ Gathering prayer:

> *Compassionate God, Peter followed Jesus from the Sea of Galilee, to the mount of transfigured glory, to the Garden of Gethsemane. Along the way, Peter learned how to listen to Jesus, pray with confidence, forgive from the heart, and wait in watchful vigilance. Help us imitate Peter as we detach ourselves from material wealth, worldly influence, and temporal security so that we may live in your kingdom, secure in the riches of your grace.*

✝ Part 1:
- Having completed the lectio divina for chapters 7–11 during the week, the group members discuss the fruit of their practice for these five chapters. Divide the chapters into equal time allotments so that no chapter is neglected. To provoke personal discussion of each chapter, ask this question: "What insight is most significant to you from your reflection on this chapter?"

✝ Part 2:
- Spend at least the last half of the group time in the full lectio divina of chapter 12. Move through each step according to the instructions provided in the chapter, leaving plenty of time for oratio, contemplatio, and operatio.

✝ Departure:
- Encourage participants to complete the lectio divina for chapters 13–17 before the next collatio group. Ask them to write their responses to each movement of lectio in their book. The lectio divina for chapter 18 will be done together in the group next week.

Collatio Group 4

✝ Gathering prayer:

> *Suffering Savior and risen Lord, you asked Peter to believe in you, to follow you, and to remain with you to prove that he is a true disciple. He learned that you alone have the words of everlasting life. Without you he failed every time, but with your presence and direction, his ministry was abundant. Teach us to imitate Peter, to wash the feet of others, to put away the sword of violence, to repent of our failures, to believe that you are risen, and to remain with you always.*

✝ Part 1:
- Having completed the lectio divina for chapters 13–17 during the week, the group members discuss the fruit of their practice for these five chapters. Divide the chapters into equal time allotments so that no chapter is neglected. To provoke personal discussion of each chapter, ask this question: "What insight is most significant to you from your reflection on this chapter?"

✝ Part 2:
- Spend at least the last half of the group time in the full lectio divina of chapter 18. Move through each step according to the instructions provided in the chapter, leaving plenty of time for oratio, contemplatio, and operatio.

✝ Departure:
- Encourage participants to complete the lectio divina for chapters 19–23 before the next collatio group. Ask them to write their responses to each movement of lectio in their book. The lectio divina for chapter 24 will be done together in the group next week.

Collatio Group 5

✝ Gathering prayer:

> *God of all nations, Peter realized that the teaching, healing, and reconciling ministry of Jesus was still alive in his church through the work of the Holy Spirit. The more he was threatened, arrested, and imprisoned, the more powerful his witness became. Give your church a missionary zeal. Help us realize that the gospel cannot be contained and that we must remove barriers to make salvation through Christ available for every person.*

✝ Part 1:
- Having completed the lectio divina for chapters 19–23 during the week, the group members discuss the fruit of their practice for these five chapters. Divide the chapters into equal time allotments so that no chapter is neglected. The most effective question to ask of each chapter is this: "What is your most important insight from this chapter?"

✝ Part 2:
- Spend at least the last half of the group time in the full lectio divina of chapter 24. Move through each step according to the instructions provided in the chapter, leaving plenty of time for oratio, contemplatio, and operatio.

✝ Departure:
- Encourage participants to complete the lectio divina for chapters 25–29 before the next collatio group. Ask them to write their responses to each movement of lectio in their book. The lectio divina for chapter 30 will be done together in the group next week.

Collatio Group 6

✝ Gathering prayer:

Lord God of all people, Peter paved the way for the gospel to go out into the entire world. He teaches that God shows no partiality toward those who treat God with reverence and people with justice. Give us a passion for the gospel and for the mission of the church. Help us believe that we are living stones in your sacred temple, that we are a royal priesthood and your chosen people. May the spiritual sacrifices of our lives always be acceptable to you as they are offered in union with the eternal sacrifice of your Son and our Savior, Jesus Christ.

✝ Part 1:
- Having completed the lectio divina for chapters 25–29 during the week, the group members discuss the fruit of their practice for these five chapters. Divide the chapters into equal time allotments so that no chapter is neglected. The most effective question to ask of each chapter is this: "What is your most important insight from this chapter?"

✝ Part 2:
- Spend at least the last half of the group time in the full lectio divina of chapter 30. Move through each step according to the instructions provided in the chapter, leaving plenty of time for oratio, contemplatio, and operatio.

✝ Departure:
- Discuss how this Ancient-Future Bible Study has made a difference in the lives of group members and whether the group wishes to study another book in the series. Consult www.brazospress.com/ancient futurebiblestudy for more study options.